John Reid

Christ and His Religion

John Reid

Christ and His Religion

ISBN/EAN: 9783337131241

Printed in Europe, USA, Canada, Australia, Japan

Cover: Foto ©Lupo / pixelio.de

More available books at **www.hansebooks.com**

CHRIST AND HIS RELIGION.

BY

REV. JOHN REID,

AUTHOR OF "VOICES OF THE SOUL ANSWERED IN GOD," ETC.

"*We must fly to our beloved fatherland. There is the Father, there our all. What fleet or flight shall convey us thither? Our way is to become like God.*"—PLOTINUS.

"*I am the way, the truth, and the life.*"—CHRIST.

NEW YORK:
ROBERT CARTER AND BROTHERS,
530 BROADWAY.
1880.

Copyright, 1880,
BY ROBERT CARTER & BROTHERS.

CAMBRIDGE:
PRESS OF
JOHN WILSON AND SON.

ST. JOHNLAND
STEREOTYPE FOUNDRY,
SUFFOLK CO., N. Y.

CONTENTS.

CHAPTER I.

CHRIST IS CHRISTIANITY.

Can not describe Christ.—His moral grandeur.—Not like the Jewish people.—Saw things as they are.—Never despises men.—Not troubled with mysteries.—His intellectual character.—Simplicity.—Devotional spirit.—No excitement.—His sweetness.—No mention of his conscience.—Great by sinking.—His meekness.—Gentleness.—Tenderness.—Self-denial.—No anxiety about eternity.—Possessed all moral traits.—Difficult to understand his character because it is finished.—He had surprises of character.—He is the only person I am satisfied with.—Always reached his ideal...................................... 11

CHAPTER II.

CHRIST IS EITHER A DIVINE SAVIOUR AND CHRISTIANITY IS TRUE, OR HE IS A DARING IMPOSTOR AND CHRISTIANITY IS FALSE.

Supernatural was natural to Christ.—His miracles not like the spurious.—Unity of his life.—Divine-human character.—Redemptive consciousness.—Idea of redemption for a world proves it divine.—The divine at times held in abeyance.—Was the last moment of Christ dark or bright? —Was there progress in his idea of redemption?—To view Christ as divine-human explains all that relates to him in the New Testament.—The holiest men are found among those who believe in his divinity.—If Christ merely a man, yet spoke as if he were God, he was an impostor.—Still, how could he be sinless, and also an impostor?—He is true God and Saviour............................ 38

CHAPTER III.

SUPERNATURAL BEGINNING OF THE RELIGION OF CHRIST IN THE SOUL.

I. Divine light for the mind.—1. A consciousness of God.—2. Of eternity.—3. Of accountability.—4. Of sin.—5. Of misery.—6. Of moral weakness.—7. Of the way to be saved.—II. Divine life for the heart.—1. This produces a holy tendency.—2. Holy taste.—3. Holy desire.—4. Holy love.—5. Spontaneity marking all these.—Use of second causes in conversion.—All holy beings have life from the spirit.—III. Divine liberty for the will.—The will by nature self-determined to evil.—A holy determination in conversion.—May be a struggle in liberating the will.—Regeneration culminates in faith.—Actions in the mind.—Character viewed as an act.................. 64

CHAPTER IV.

MORALITY AND THE RELIGION OF CHRIST AS DISTINGUISHED FROM EACH OTHER.

First, what is implied in morality?—1. An idea of a moral law.—2. A feeling of obligation to keep the law.—3. An attempt to keep the law.—Secondly, what is implied in religion?—1. An idea of God.—2. A feeling of union with God through Christ.—3. Complete self-devotement to God through Christ.—Morality has no element that satisfies the law.—Religion is redemptive.—Contrast between Dr. Gorden the moralist and Dr. Gorden the Christian.—Sceptical element in morality.—Attempt to trust in morality and also in God................................ 89

CHAPTER V.

ETHICS OF CHRIST AS THEY CHARACTERIZE HIS RELIGION.

Leading systems of human ethics can be traced to leading faculties of the mind.—Christian ethics demand a right

state of heart.—Love to God.—Love to Christ.—Humility.
—Not a system, but principles.—Perfection in a person
rather than in an ideal.—Obligation deepened by ethics
of Christ.—Motives multiplied.—Christian ethics the ideal
ethics 104

CHAPTER VI.

WORSHIP AS A CENTRAL FEATURE OF THE RELIGION OF CHRIST.

Simplicity of Christian worship.—Vivid conception of God
necessary to right worship.—Preaching tends to produce
this.—Also thoughtful reading of Scripture.—Worship redemptive.—Christian emotions find their outlet in worship.—Prayer distinct and burdensome.—Awe and freedom in it.—Praise.—Worship not a means, but an end.—
Music.. 122

CHAPTER VII.

DECAY IN THE RELIGION OF CHRIST FROM CAUSES IN HUMAN NATURE.

I. Decay from evils of the heart.—1. From indifference.—2.
Love of ease.—3. Carelessness.—4. Attractive sin.—5. Secular spirit.—6. Wayward imagination.—7. Besetting sin.
—8. Want of simplicity.—9. Not acting out pure feelings.—10. The enmity of sin.—II. Decay from errors of
the mind.—1. From misguided mental enthusiasm.—2.
False philosophy.—3. Mere abstract thinking.—4. Reverence for secondary things.—5. Diplomatic piety.—6. Allowing unconverted men to unite with the Church.—
III. Decay from a deceived conscience.—1. Conscience
deceived by ignorance.—2. By natural traits which resemble the spiritual.—3. By prejudice.—4. By near relationship.—5. By evil habit.—6. By tenacity in holding on to
a wrong opinion.—7. By selfishness.—8. By presenting
a good reason when a bad one governs.—9. By following a first impulse.—10. By following a cool judgment.—
11. By good running into evil........................... 144

CHAPTER VIII.

MEANS TO ARREST DECAY IN THE RELIGION OF CHRIST.

I. A view of the piety of the early Christians a means to arrest decay in religion.—Their piety characterized by love.—Simplicity.—Firm persuasion of the truth.—Steadfastness.—Christly element.—Cheerfulness.—A critical estimate of their character.—The mind inspired by it.—II. Direct method of arresting decay in religion.—Recalling a bright past-vivid conception of truth.—Reproduction of our first experience.—Cultivating the power to receive.—The power to form.—Principle governing...... 167

CHAPTER IX.

LAWS OF PROGRESS IN THE RELIGION OF CHRIST.

First law of progress: development through the medium of groups.—Second law of progress: development threefold.—Third law of progress: development by epochs.—Fourth law of progress: development antithetic.—Fifth law of progress: development from fewness to manifoldness.... 197

CHAPTER X.

TO ADVANCE IN THE RELIGION OF CHRIST DEMANDS STRENUOUS EFFORT.

A law of limitation in the bestowment of divine grace, making it necessary to struggle.—Profit and pleasure powers in earthly life, but not in religion.—Must work through pain.—Must do what we do not want to do.—Must not be irritated.—Must overcome temptation.—Cultivate moral indignation.—Also courage.—Must benefit others with what we have.—Must have the religion of missions.—Church to represent the life of Christ................ 218

CHAPTER XI.

DISCIPLINE BEST EFFECTED IN THE RELIGION OF CHRIST BY THOROUGHNESS IN ONE OR TWO THINGS.

The thought illustrated in the training of the intellect.—Applied to the formation of Christian character.—First, a substantial character formed by thoroughness in the doctrines of sin and of God.—Secondly, by the development of leading states of mind.—As in the sense of the infinite, the consciousness of salvation, and the habit of self-forgetfulness.—While the Bible looks to various duties, it depends mainly on moral states.—In all false religions the attention fixed on a round of services................ 236

CHAPTER XII.

NON-VOLUNTARY INFLUENCE AS AFFECTING THE RELIGION OF CHRIST.

Religion affected by nature.—Temperament.—Hunger.—The countenance.—Passive virtues.—Laws of association.—Home.—Trouble.—Death.—A graveyard.—The inevitable.—A spiritual atmosphere.......................... 254

CHAPTER XIII.

CONCEALED GREATNESS AN ADVANCED PHASE OF THE RELIGION OF CHRIST.

Three grades of pious men: the inferior, the medium, the superior.—Hidden intellectual life.—Hidden religious life.—Our feelings, repentings, and aspirations not seen.—Great power may come from the untold wealth of a deeply pious mind.—Success not measured by what we see.—Inward repose.—Character not complete that is formed by facts.—Ideal element needed.—An experience so deep that it shades off into the indefinite.—Danger that outward goodness will make one lose sight of the inner life.—Christ far greater than he seemed to be ... 279

CHAPTER XIV.

BLESSEDNESS AS FLOWING FROM THE RELIGION OF CHRIST

I. Blessedness from right emotion.—From the sense of freedom.—The working of love.—Singleness of the spiritual.—The divine in character.—II. Blessedness from right activity.—The unoccupied mind restless.—Our joy does not have the proper relish because activity not full volumed.—III. Blessedness from right passivity. Passive states of goodness.—We look forward to a season of repose.—I must be able to find peace by facing the soul.—Eternal toil not the ultimate life.—There is a sabbath of mind.—IV. Blessedness from the attainment of a right end.—The thought hinted at in nature.—Joy because the great question of life is settled.—Joy from pardon.—We have delight when a noble work is finished.—To find the permanent is to rest.—V. Blessedness from a right state of oneness.—To detect a principle of unity is satisfying.—Blessedness springs from oneness with self.—Oneness with God.—Oneness with the holy intelligences of heaven........ 303

CHRIST AND HIS RELIGION.

CHAPTER I.

CHRIST IS CHRISTIANITY.

THERE is floating around at present what may be called the religion of admiration. This admiration is awakened by the excellencies of Christ and his religion. The entire mind of Christendom has been elevated by the continuous presence of a great person and a great life. Even sceptical men see a glory which they praise, and earthly men see a heavenliness which makes them sigh. There is a class of ultimate conceptions in Christianity, not abstract, but with form and life, and these charm the creaturely mind. The idea of *order* is called out by the sight of absolute harmony. We seem to be looking at the working of God, and seem to be hearing the words of the divine language. The thought of the *limitless* strikes us with new power. During one moment our nature is expanded, while during the next moment we sink into nothingness. The Man of men appears to us as the ultimate Being. His shadow protects us. In his presence we are silent. Thoughtful respecting his nature, we advance. Life comes to us from his heart.

All about Christ is striking. We have to escape from ourselves in order to find him. In a prosaic manner we can not reach his life. We have to think of him ideally, as well as through the medium of a spiritual understanding, in order to approach somewhat his actual existence. At the best we never stand beside him and see across his wonderful movements. There is before us a great ocean; and only a part of it have we explored. We may think of Christ all our days, and at the close of them know but little about him. He is a sea that never has been sounded. That sea is the Pacific of the universe. It is the great ocean of God. No storms break over it. No conflicting currents press through it. Night does not darken it. Clouds do not overhang it. The light of a divine day sparkles on its bosom. Its motion reminds one of a blessedness that is complete.

There was a *moral grandeur* about the life of Christ. It makes no difference in what circumstances we find him—painful or pleasant, with the rich or the poor, with the ignorant or the educated—his moral grandeur never departs. He does not leap into a state of *abandon*, as sometimes the best of men will do, neither is there an air of pomp or stiffness surrounding him. He does not find it necessary to stand upon his dignity, and yet he is never lawless in his manner. There is nothing of the eccentric about him. He never uttered words which brought down the house in a roar of laughter. The majesty of Christ is the majesty of absolute truth and absolute righteousness. The glory of his character seems like the morning of heaven; as if the blessedness of God had found a home in his heart, and the beauty of God were seen in every part of his being.

It is an entrancing sight to see the moon come forth from the summit of a snow-capped mountain, or to see it rise out of the ocean on the verge of the horizon, or to behold it burst forth from the midst of dark and angry clouds. Christ rises in this way out of the midst of an obstinate and perverted race. Though a Jew, he seems not to belong to that people. His language, figures of speech, form of worship, and a few other characteristics, are about all that mark him off as strictly Jewish. He had a spontaneity of development that never has been seen in any mere man. There were no extrinsic follies hanging around him,—no whims, prejudices, or superstitions.

Christ did many things that horrified the Jewish people. He seemed to them to be a great deceiver; one that was doing his best to lead men to destruction; one that must be watched, secured, and condemned. Then what strange truth he announced in their hearing! How they were startled by it! How many times they were enraged! How they grew worse instead of better under his preaching! Even some of his professed disciples would leave him, thinking that he was unreasonable; that he was doing evil instead of good; that he did not understand the signs of the times; that he did not seem to know the people among whom he lived. There was a great deal of secret as well as public murmuring in regard to his ways, showing that he did not harmonize with the men of his own land and time.

Christ had the faculty of seeing things *as they are.* He did not rest with appearances. He lived in the midst of the real. Men and things stood right before him: he could see them with a kind of direct vision. This was not the case with him during some favored hour: all through the hours his eye was fastened on the real. Men might come to him with great art intending to entrap him, but with a single glance he sees through their manner and their schemes. That which gave weight to all that Christ spoke with reference to the character of men, was the fact that he did not view them as they appeared to be, but as they were in their *heart.* This dealing with *real persons*, and not with persons as they were silvered over for the occasion, startled many, and broke through the conventionalisms of society.

Christ looked at every thing in this realistic way. All kinds of thoughts came forth from their hiding places; came forth trembling into the light; and he saw them and announced them with all the sharpness of their identity. No doubt the crowds of curious people who gathered around him were frequently searched as they heard his direct statements. He must have seemed to many of them as a prophet of God. When he spoke of sin and holiness, death and judgment, heaven and hell, how much they meant! Souls and subjects seemed to be dissected by him. It is no wonder that "the people marvelled greatly."

Although Christ looked straight into souls, and of course saw a great deal of wickedness, he is *never misanthropic*. In every possible way men tried to entrap him, manifesting hypocrisy and deadly hate, yet no symptom of ill-will appears on his part. Some truly pious persons are apt to look with contempt on certain classes. It is not easy to treat respectfully the fickle multitude with their follies and spites, the underhanded with their pretence of fairness, the great men who are small, the ignorant who are proud, the friend who becomes an enemy. It is true that Christ hated sin; hated it as no man ever did; but he could do that without having any feeling of malice against the sinner. No mere outward obeisance did he pay to the wicked, while enmity lurked in his heart. He never tried to catch men by appealing to their weaknesses, that he might scorn them after they had been beguiled by his subtilty. He honored all because of their relation to God and immortality. He had no feeling of caste. He could mingle with publicans and sinners in order to benefit them. The poor and illiterate children of God he welcomed as warmly as he did the rich and the educated disciples.

Men who have reached any maturity of intellect are troubled more or less with the *mysterious things* which belong to the divine system. There are seeming confusions that we can not harmonize, and apparent contradictions that we can not reconcile. The mind therefore wanders as one who has lost his way, and doubts by reason of the strange things which strike the soul. Wrong feelings arise in the heart; perplexity torments the understanding; unhappiness eats into the troubled spirit. Now, nothing of this kind of experience is seen in Christ. He seems to have been able to look over the system of God, finding nothing in that system that threw him into a state of doubt. Where to us there is intricacy, to him there was plainness. He had the faculty of generalization as we have not. He could seize upon a principle of unity that gathered up into itself facts and truths that we either do not see, or do not understand when we do see. The intuition and grasp of a sinless mind are very different from the same traits in a mind that is fallen. The logic of holiness is a great harmonizer, while sin is a great divider. Christ did not attempt to explain away the dark features of the creation as some wise men have attempted to do, hoping by such means to find rest. If sin and misery are puzzles, he does not try to lessen the misery by lessening the sin. He rather holds up to view the exceeding malice of depravity, and intensifies the mental pain instead of weakening it. His high attitude of life, standing on the mountain summit of being, while we are away down in the valleys below, enabled him to take in a multitude of particulars, which, if we could behold them, would quiet us, even as they quieted him. If we had the character and standpoint of Jesus, our perplexities would give way to his peace: faith would rest in a wisdom that is divine, and in a goodness that is perfect.

There was a *mental character* to Christ that was peculiar to himself. Though mingling with men, he seemed to have made his home among the stars; breathed there the atmosphere of God; was therefore touched by divine powers; his understanding in this way receiving a purity that stamped it with singularity, causing it to be out of the plane of even the best minds of the race. He had laws of association that connected themselves with the higher worlds of existence; and these same laws fastening themselves to the earth and man, started trains of thinking that had all around them a celestial radiance. His attachment to the whole range of truth threw a sanctity over his understanding, as if that same understanding had been formed out of the eternal ideas, the archetypes of the creation seeming there to be at home. It is evident also that the poetical mind belonged to Christ. Not merely do we see this poetical mind in the parables which he uttered, but in the rhythm of his common language, in the harmony of his thoughts, and in the music that chanted through his life. His soul seemed to be a poem; a poem that related to God and man, to time and eternity; having in it the deep wail of grief, and the heaven of joy.

There is a beautiful *simplicity* in the character of Christ. Nothing appears that is forced. There is a certain freedom and ease that strike one favorably. His varied perfections have as much naturalness about them as the fruit of a tree. His single aim, which ran through the whole of his life, made his character to be definite and unmixed. Although he may appear strange to us, he never appears strange to himself. He never goes so far in goodness as to astonish himself. He has no favored hour during which he performs a class of duties that are remembered ever after as out of the range of his common life. The virtues of Jesus stream forth from his soul with as much beauty and power as the rays of light stream forth from the sun. In fact his character has such singleness and delicacy that we think of it as formed out of the unbroken rays of light. There is an ethereal cast to it which reminds us of heaven and of God.

His soul is always in a *devotional state.* He never loses this by extraordinary cares and labors. Whether he works or worships the devotional spirit is always fresh and fervent. To commune with God was the normal state of his being. A night in prayer was only a chapter of that volume of supplication which was uttered by his heart during all the days of his life. Whether in synagogue, or by the rushing waters of Jordan; among the busy crowds of men, or in the deep solitudes of the desert; in the humble dwellings of the poor, or dying in agony on the cross—prayer ascended from his soul as the vapor ascends from the infinite sea. No cry ever entered heaven like that which Jesus uttered, and no answer ever came down to bless men like that which followed his supplication. As he had no sins of his own that needed forgiveness, he could only ask that pardon might be extended to others. His prayer always went clear up to God; never hindered by doubts and fears. His dependence was complete; death could not shake it. The echoes of his prayer even now seem to be sounding through our souls, and answers come down upon us like the dew that falls upon the hill of Zion. On the stormy days of life some favored message may reach us, as if a postman had come with it from the climes of God. Christ's soul is full of prayers for us all, and tokens of his love may reach us before we pass away.

The life of Jesus was not struck upon a high key of excitement. There was courage, power, majesty; but nothing of the feverish and the eruptive. It was not monotonous and tame. There were hills and valleys to diversify it; then straight pathways, with flowers and trees of life planted on either side of them. No doubt there was fire in the character of Christ, a divine flame, but it was finely controlled. He does not dash off with impetuosity one hour, and sink into languor the next. He was earnest without being fierce, and calm without being dull. No one could think of him as a mere religious enthusiast. He is always master of himself, and master of the situation in which he may be placed. There were times when he seemed to be terrible with justice, but the terribleness was divine. In his style of address there was nothing of the flaming orator. There was power, but it was as near as possible the simple power of truth and goodness: as if Truth and Goodness themselves were speaking. Whatever he may be doing and whatever he may be saying, he never exhausts the spiritual contents of his being.

There was a certain *sweetness* about Jesus which gave a coloring and character to all that he did. Men are apt to emphasize their great efforts: Christ marched forward very much like God. "He did not strive nor cry, neither was his voice heard in the streets." Persons "wondered at the gracious words which proceeded out of his mouth." We can not speak of Christ as being either saintly or seraphic. His righteousness had all the peculiarity of his own nature. To say that he was a great religious genius has no meaning: as well say that he was a great religious naturalist. There was nothing of the ascetic about him: he was a veritable man among men. Sanctimoniousness does not appear in his character. He does not play with pious words. He was not distant and morose; yet to say that he was genial would not express the exact truth. There was a *something* about him which gave character to all his actions; and that something we do not possess. He lived in an atmosphere that does not surround us. He seems like a wondrous cloud that had come from the skies of eternity. Some parts are exceedingly radiant with heavenly glory, so that palaces of light can be seen in it, as if they were the habitations of the angels or the homes of the saved. Other parts are soft and serene with the chaste beauty of a morning in spring, when the air is full of life and full of peace. A healing power seems to be all about it as if the virtues of God crowned it, and then dropped down lightly upon souls as the dew upon herbs. Wherever this cloud goes there is health. The fainting spirit by it is quickened, and the disconsolate soul made glad. The gentle rain descends from it like that which falls in heaven; making each heart to be a garden of the Lord, with fruit trees bearing fruit, and flowers fragrant with the odors of love. On the scorching days of time the weary dwell under its shadow, and are bathed as in a celestial fountain of life. Its grandeur never departs, neither does its beauty become less. It is the joy of souls, and the treasury of all that is good.

No writer of the Bible speaks of the *conscience* of Christ. We should have supposed that one who acted with such purity would have had his conscience stand out like a star in the darkness, or like a lighthouse on a rock amid the dangers of night. But, perhaps, a reason for this omission is found in the very nature of Christ's activity. He does not seem to act so much from his conscience as from his *heart*. His whole life upon earth is to be explained upon the principle of love. It was not mere duty that brought him here and that kept him here, but it was the transcendent power of a benevolent affection. He stands forth as supremely great, because he manifested a love which no one else could manifest. A burden rested upon him which no one else could carry. The love was so disinterested that it took the body and soul of Christ and delivered them up as a sacrifice to God.

There was a greatness in him that resulted from *sinking*, rather than from rising. When a man by continuous effort ascends from a low position in life to one that is high, we are accustomed to call such a person great. In fact that is the usual way that men become great among us. The greatness of Christ, however, consisted in going down; and according to the depth of his descent, was seen the height of his greatness. We may contemplate his whole life as but one continuous act of condescension. He was great also by attending to small things: men deem themselves great by attending to great things. Real greatness is not seen unless the soul of it is humility. The sovereign who becomes a slave is greater than the slave who becomes a sovereign. To be a kingly man is nobler than for a man to be a king.

A considerable amount of Christ's character was summed up in his *meekness*. There is a difficulty in attempting to represent any of the excellencies of his life, because the best of our earthly words which express these excellencies are below the standard. These best words are applied to certain classes of men; men who are never complete in any grace whatsoever. Suppose I say of one man that he is courageous, of another that he is truthful, and then of another that he is meek—all this is to be received in a way of human limitation; for the courage, truthfulness, and meekness have the shadow of sin thrown over them. The language of heaven, as that describes any phase of goodness, must have a wealth of meaning that is not found in the language of earth. We must see to it, then, that when we speak of the meekness of Christ, or any other trait of his character, we view it as far above any earthly sample that may be called by the same name. That which we call meekness in Jesus is not so much a single characteristic, as it is a compound of beauties, an extended moral state, a gem that sparkles with many colors. When we start with the idea that Christ was meek, we picture to ourselves a countenance that was radiant with the soft light of an eternal morning. We always remember that Jesus had sorrow, and that his countenance made known that fact. His meekness, therefore, had a casting of grief, as when the sun goes down in the midst of blue clouds.

There must have been a peculiar expression about his eye. The image of meekness must have been seen there as in a glass. As a living soul it lived there as in a refined body: it was there incarnate.

We think also of the *gentleness* of Christ; a fine characteristic in one that was so great. He had no rough thought, no rough feeling, no rough choice. There was nothing that might be called overbearing about him: his gentleness forbade that. There are men who pride themselves in their independence. They wish to think for themselves, mean to stand up for their rights, are not afraid to speak their mind. But such characters are apt to go a little too far. Their towering independence is a little too sharp and defiant. Gentleness can not grow under its shadow. The most timid might approach Christ. A child could take him by the hand. There was nothing repelling about him. It was the nature of his soul to draw, the nature of his manner to draw, the nature of his appearance to draw.

We must not fail to notice also the *tenderness* of Jesus. His tenderness was not a perfected sample of pity. It was higher and purer than any refined movement of instinctive feeling. It belonged to a region of mind that was most holy. It was embosomed in mercy. Its speech was hope, and its benediction peace. The tenderness of Jesus had no frown. It was not pity on the lips while there was a scowl on the heart. But it was a tenderness which warmed, softened, and saved. It is because of this winning characteristic that wandering men kneel down at the cross. The little child prays and trusts because of this. The despairing man by it gains hope, and the weary man by it gains strength. The tenderness of Jesus is like a gateway of love that opens into the kingdom of grace; like an angel of love that guides us through the night of time, leaving us not till we have reached the day of God.

Christ had the great virtue of *self-denial*. In fact it was not a virtue, not a grace—it was rather his collective goodness taking the form of self-sacrifice. He had not struck out a course of existence that was easy and pleasant. We can think of a ship sailing along a peaceful sea with a fair wind, of a stream flowing onward through a channel with no impediment, of a sun shining during a beautiful day with the fields enamelled with green and the sky with blue—and all such pictures giving us the idea of ease. We can even think of angels at their morning worship in the temple of heaven, of glorified men walking along by the river of God, of bright celestial companies gliding through space to distant worlds—and all this, though in the strict line of duty, pleasant and easy. Now, it is not in any such way as this that we are to view the position of Christ upon earth. He did not come among us as a traveller, intending to study the manners, customs, and history of a strange people; did not even come as an ambassador from the court of God, proposing terms of peace to a rebellious province of his empire; but he came as a Sufferer. If the strange contrast of purity and pain is not seen in his life, nothing is seen.

Christ had *not the least anxiety* with reference to *eternity*. All men are more or less anxious touching the tremendous possibilities of the eternal state. Special efforts have been made to drive away fear as it respects the future; but the efforts are not successful.

So long as man is a sinner and God is just, there will be fear. It is worthy of note, then, that we find one person, and but one, who had no anxiety during any moment of life in regard to the retributions of eternity. How could he fear when he had no sense of guilt? He had not the least feeling of unworthiness: the very best men have that feeling. The past did not cause him to grieve, and the future did not cause him to tremble. Surely his character was unlike that of all other men.

Christ did not merely have *one* leading moral trait, like the chief minds of the past, but he had *all* the moral traits. He was not one-sided. His character does not show strength and weakness, beauties and deformities. In the working of his *intellect*, he is never at fault. There is no false statement, no false reasoning. He does not find it necessary to change his opinions by reason of new light. Although his thoughts are exceedingly comprehensive, entering into a region where men have not been accustomed to go, he yet finds them all sure. Even up to this late day no improvement can be made upon his teaching. In the working of his *feelings*, there is no wrong movement. The right emotion always appears in the right circumstances. The feelings are neither too fast nor too slow. Their measure and variety are just as they should be. In the working of Christ's *will*, there is no hindering power. It always has a ready and fixed determination for righteousness. The entire will, and not a part of it, is set for that which is good. Thus we may speak of the whole mind of Jesus as true, pure, beautiful. As the various colors blend together and constitute light, so the various virtues blend together and constitute love.

A difficulty which hinders us from grasping the character of Christ is the fact that the character is *finished*. Our character is unfinished at every point. There is not a single faculty that works in a normal way; not a single grace that is complete in itself; not one good habit or good tendency that is just as it should be,—consequently we are in no condition to see Christ as he stands before us in his peerless perfection. We see him, and yet we do not see him. Only a part of his nature strikes us, because only a part of our nature bears a feeble resemblance to it. No one but a finished painter can judge of a finished painting. Only he who has a genius for poetry can detect the excellencies of a poem. If I would know goodness I must be good. It takes Christ to see Christ. We can judge of pious men with a fair degree of truthfulness, because these pious men have but one or two marked traits of character. The marked traits make them stand out; while perfection being a single glory it does not startle us so much. The love of John and the philanthropy of Howard arrest our attention.

It must be confessed, however, that there are *surprises of character* about Christ. We can not understand why the eighteen Christian centuries should have fixed their gaze upon this one person, if he did not possess features of goodness that struck men with surprise. His complete disinterestedness stands out like a sun, and his death is such a marvel that it never can be forgotten. There were Alps of goodness about him, rivers of purity beautiful as the Rhine, cities of righteousness with their palaces of love, that are always remembered with joy. In fact he seems like a Holy Land with its mountains and sea, its plain of Esdraelon and Jordan Valley, its Jerusalem with the temple of God, its Bethlehem where first he appeared, and its Calvary where at last he went away.

Christ is the only person upon earth with whom I am *satisfied*. I think of him with the utmost pleasure. I find nothing in him that jars upon my soul; nothing that clashes with my sense of right. He knew nothing of unrest, although he knew what it was to suffer pain. The pain to him was foreign; it came from without. His state of repose sprang from within; it was the result of purity. Upon whatever men I gaze, they are evil and restless. I may think of the past, the brightest and best ages of the past, I yet can find no human being upon whom I can look with complete satisfaction. I look to Jesus. I can not say he could be better at any point. Only with him am I satisfied. He seems like a majestic river that is winding its way through time, having come from the lands of eternity. Yea, he seems like a great world of light,—a new sun that has appeared in the spaces of God,—the centre of a new system, nobler and better than all others. Although sixty-two generations of men have passed away since Christ appeared, he has never been reproduced; neither can we imagine any advanced thought or action in the future ages that will give to us a second Christ. He is out of the range of the world's movement. He is not swept onward by the winds and waves that sweep us along. The glories of heaven radiate around his Spirit, and he tarries among us as one whose home is in the bosom of God. With outstretched hands he blesses the whole race of man, and then departs. His benediction still rests upon us, and his image goes with us in all our journey of toil.

That which arrests the attention of a thoughtful observer is the singular fact—Christ *always reached his ideal.* He stands forth as a new character in human history. Although in appearance he is like us, in reality he is not of us. The plane of his life is out of our range. He passes by among us as one who has come from afar; as one on his way to the worlds of light from which he came. He is the voice of Goodness; the psalm of God. He is the

Head of a new race of men; the crown and glory of the creation. Not a single human being has ever reached his ideal. All have the consciousness of sin; all have guilt; all have remorse. Men everywhere are dissatisfied. Whether the race should exist thousands or millions of years, it will still be true that each member of the race will sink beneath his ideal. Christ stands alone during the whole sweep of time. He did not grow up from sin to holiness: he was pure from the very beginning of life. Regrets and vain desires he had not. He shows no symptom of wounded pride. He does not chafe in his soul. He makes no pretence. He is surrounded with many disadvantages; bad circumstances seem to blacken him; yet he manifests no uneasiness of mind because men will judge him unfavorably from these unfavorable circumstances. Shame because of a bad environment is not seen. No hints are thrown out as if he would say, I am sorry that you find me thus. I hope you will not judge me by these untoward appearances. I was once in a better state than the one in which you now see me. All such human contrivances to court a name are never thought of. Jesus puts on no airs, does nothing for effect, is never chagrined; but conscious of a pure spiritual existence, he lives and loves as if he were inhabiting the city of God, with principalities and powers all about him. That he should thus be the one personality who has never fallen below his ideal—this has a divine meaning. If he is of the race, why is he not like the race? He is either a sinner, or he is greater than a sinless man.

CHAPTER II.

CHRIST IS EITHER A DIVINE SAVIOUR AND CHRISTIANITY IS TRUE, OR HE IS A DARING IMPOSTOR AND CHRISTIANITY IS FALSE.

THE *supernatural* with Christ was *natural*. In the course of his journeys from place to place he meets the sick and heals them. He does this in the most natural way. No special effort seems to be made. A blind man asks that his eyes may be opened: Christ opens them. A funeral procession is passing by; he stops it; he raises the dead. A word is spoken very much as he would speak any word, and the result follows. At a particular time thousands of people follow him. Knowing that they are both hungry and weary, he asks them to be seated. Finding a few loaves and fishes, he invokes the divine blessing, and then distributes them to the multitude. Each person eats, and each is satisfied. Here there is no great ado. We only notice that the supernatural was quite natural to

Christ. He is not found at any time unprepared for this kind of work. He is never brought to a stand, as if he did not know what to do in given circumstances. Even in regard to all the variety of diseases that he is asked to cure, he has not to examine each case with critical skill that he may know how to treat it. He simply speaks the word, and the person is healed; is healed at once. Certainly this way of acting has a divine look to it. Christ does not with great shrewdness arrange matters so as to startle the people. An impostor would want to overwhelm them by what seemed like a dash of the supernatural. If forged miracles had been introduced into the Christian records, they would not have been of the kind we now find there. The miracle life of Christ is altogether too hidden to suit the taste of a forger.

If we just note two or three Roman Catholic miracles, we shall see how they differ from those of Jesus. As St. Elizabeth, of Hungary, was one time carrying bread, meat, and eggs, to the poor, she was met by her husband. He being anxious to see what she carried, drew open her mantle. When lo!

the bread, meat, and eggs were changed into red and white roses; the most beautiful he had ever seen! This astonished him greatly, as it was not the season of flowers. He took one of the roses, which he preserved all his life. At another time a company of noblemen came to visit Elizabeth. She had no robes with which she could suitably appear in their presence, and there was no time to prepare new ones Praying to God to make her agreeable to her friends, she was at once introduced to them. When, to the great surprise of the duke, and the admiration of those with him, "she appeared clothed in magnificent silken robes, and covered with a mantle of azure velvet, embroidered with pearls of great price!" Another story informs us that Elizabeth once took care of a leper, who was so diseased that no one would venture to approach him. She anointed him with balm, and laid him in her own bed. Her husband hearing of this was irritated. Entering the room where the leper was found, and going up to the bed, whom should he see? Not the leper at all; but *Jesus Christ!* *

---

* De Montalembert's "Life of St. Elizabeth," pp. 155, 181.

Miracles like these are seen to be spurious at a glance, and are just of that kind that we might expect from a forger. With Jesus, miracles never look as if they were far-fetched. They are not like divine wonders glued on to his life. We simply behold "the Lord of glory" walking among men, and acting always like himself. His life is not according to any human theory. He outwits all human invention. If Jesus had been dressed up to suit the fevered imagination of ignorant and superstitious followers, the great facts of unity and harmony that now are seen in his life would be seen no more. A startling miracle would be fastened on to him here, and another there; very much as the Oriental female is decorated with ear-rings and nose-jewels,—these being no part of the living body. If the miracles of Christ were a kind of fancy waxwork stuck on to his life, why, in that case we could remove them; and his real life would be freer and fresher without such foreign appendages. But let any one go through the gospels in this way, and with his finely prepared instruments separate the miracles from the life of our Lord,—what follows? Why, Christ is dead at once; no Christ is left. One might take hold of Roman Catholic saints, and strike off the miracles that are attached to them, with great benefit to the persons concerned; but not so with Jesus. The supernatural with him is so natural, is so much a part and parcel of himself, that it is absolutely impossible to remove it. We must either take him altogether, or reject him altogether. There is no middle ground to stand on.

"A distinct INDIVIDUALITY," says Isaac Taylor, "presents itself in the perusal of the four gospels: all the world feels this, and has felt it in every age. By the consent of mankind, or the involuntary suffrage of Christianized nations, ancient and modern, a perfect individual idea, combining the intellectual and moral qualities of ONE who is wise and good, and who is possessed of superhuman power and authority, is embodied in the four gospels. This harmony, or, as we call it, beauty of character, in which there is no distortion, and with which nothing is mingled that is incoherent, is spread over the entire surface of the evangelic narratives, embracing the supernatural incidents of the life of Christ, not less than the natural. In these narratives no seams, or joints, can be discerned, shining where the spurious portion has been spliced on to the genuine."*

That Christ has a *divine-human character* is plain from the gospel history. To confine his character to his human soul, however large and pure that soul might be, is not possible. As a theanthropic person, you hear him using such language as this: "Where two or three are gathered together in my name, there am I in the midst of them." "I have power to lay down my life, and I have power to take it again." "Destroy this temple, and in three days I will raise it up." "Before Abraham was, I am." No man ever would speak thus. The language implies divine-human character. The *central position* which Christ assumes, compels us to view him as God-man. No one is to approach the Father except through him; and he demands that every one should honor him even as they honor the Father. He says, "Whatsoever ye shall ask in my name, I will do

* "The Restoration of Belief," p. 226.

it,"—even to the sending of the Eternal Spirit himself. Thus the treasury of the Godhead is open to him, and he dispenses infinite favors according to the sovereignty of his own will. Without any limitation whatsoever, he says to all men: "Without me ye can do nothing:" he proclaims the wondrous fact that he is to raise the dead, and judge the world. We stand appalled before such a Presence. "Never man spake like this man." "Truly this is the Son of God." "The bare fact," says Ullman, "that a Being actually appeared who, on the one hand, assumed such a position with respect to God and a higher world, and, on the other hand, displayed such mental and moral sublimity, is inexplicable, on moral or psychological grounds, unless this position to God and a higher world be a true and genuine fact." *

If there be any thing certain about the Christ of history, it is certain that he lived a divine-human life. It does not require any critical skill to seize and present the divine-human elements. They are patent to each mind; and it is for this very reason

---

* "The Sinlessness of Jesus," p. 199.

that the Church, with such marked unanimity, receives Christ as God-man. The idea of classifying Christ among men, as one of their number, living within the strict range of their life, or, at least, as manifesting their highest form of religious thinking and action—the idea of doing that is just out of the question; it is a moral impossibility. It is like a man trying to go straight ahead, bound to go straight ahead, when all at once he strikes against a great rock, and is not able to proceed. The divine-human features of Christ are too many and distinct, to think about viewing him as merely a very pious man, a notable Jew that was somewhat ahead of his time. A person who can say of himself that he is "the Lord of the sabbath," "the Light of the world," the one Son who knows the eternal Father, is not in a line with man at all. To be scanning the human nature of Christ, enlarging it as much as we can, refining it as much as we can, is to work at the wrong end. We are not to begin with Christ as man, and then go up to God; but we are to begin with Christ as God, and then come down to man. The divine is the first and chief. It was the eternal Logos that became flesh, and dwelt among us. The personality is divine, and not human. Looking at Christ in this way all is clear. He is seen as he is.

We take now another step in our argument: Christ has a *redemptive consciousness*, and, by having that, shows that he is *the divine-human Saviour*. This redemptive consciousness found expression in the words: "Thy sins be forgiven thee"; "Come unto me, all ye that labor and are heavy laden, and I will give you rest"; "I lay down my life for the sheep." Or with still greater clearness in this verse: "He gave his life a *ransom* for many." The Greek word translated ransom is *lutron;* meaning a redemption-price. Christ gave his life as the redemption-price for men. We find that captives and slaves were redeemed by the payment of a price. A slave also by his own labor might redeem himself. The labor in that case was the *lutron*. As we look into the Septuagint, we find the same usage in regard to this Greek word. Ex. xxi. 30, reads thus: "If there be laid on him a sum of money, then he shall give for the *ransom* of his life whatsoever is laid upon him." Here ransom is *lutra;* the word being in the plural, and still meaning redemption-price. In Ex. xxx. 12, we have this language: "When thou takest the sum of the children of Israel after their number, then shall they give every man a *ransom* for his soul unto the Lord." The ransom again is *lutra.* In Num. xxxv. 31, this command is given: "Ye shall take no *satisfaction* for the life of a murderer, which is guilty of death." Satisfaction in this place is the same as the *lutra* of the Greek.

These passages show the meaning of the word. The meaning was well understood. As to the apostolic understanding of *lutron*, that is quite definite. Peter says: "Ye are not *redeemed* with corruptible things as silver and gold, but with the precious blood of Christ." The redemption-price of souls is not money, but blood. Paul says: "Christ hath *redeemed* us from the curse of the law, being made a curse for us." And John echoes the same redemptive thought in these words: "Thou wast slain, and hast *redeemed* us to God by thy blood." In two of these passages the word translated *redeemed* means *bought;* a word quite as expressive as the strictly redemptive one, and even showing us how it was used. As presenting the same idea, we have this passage: "Ye are not your own; for ye are *bought* with a price: therefore glorify God in your body and in your spirit, which are God's."

Thus Christ is a *Redeemer.* The redemptive theology of the New Testament never could have had an existence save as Christ revealed it himself. It is safe to affirm that the Jewish mind, at the time when Christ appeared, had no idea of a redemption for the race by the blood of a divine man. The apostles themselves were exceedingly slow in learning the doctrine. They only saw it, in its rounded form, after the death of Jesus, and after he had explained it to them with greater particularity than usual. In fact the idea of an incarnate Redeemer, as finding a place in the world's thinking at the time it did, is evidence that the idea came from God; for no man untaught by Christ knew any thing about it. There was no development at work that could produce the idea. It could no more have arisen at that time than the conception of the electric telegraph. That Christ is a divine-human person, and a divine-human Redeemer, are thoughts whose very existence prove their soundness. Neither the one nor the other came forth from the soul of man. Christ, then, is a great representative character; the Mediator between God and men; the Saviour of sinners. Even viewed as the pre-existent Logos, there was a phase of the redemptive about him. He had agreed to come as the Redeemer. He saw what he must be, do, suffer, and was ready for the great task. Then as the angel of Jehovah, acting a part during the pre-Christian centuries, we see intimations of redemption coming forth from him. Chiefly, however, when he became man was he redemptive. His humanity was not on the same plane as the Adamic humanity; nor even on the same plane as the ideal humanity. He was wholly a redemptive character; standing alone amidst the generations of time; standing alone amidst all creaturely existence. He is "the Lamb slain from the foundation of the world." The very earth was created and fitted up in view of redemption. The entire history of the race is redemptive. The God-man is the centre of the world's hopes. Life has no meaning without him. Christ is salvation.

There is a phase of the redemptive consciousness of Christ which must be noticed; I refer to the fact that the *divine* in him was, at times, *held in abeyance*. There is an extreme view which affirms that the divinity of the Saviour was entirely repressed during his stay upon earth. There is no evidence of this. Not the least change took place in the Logos when he assumed our nature; nor did the least change take place afterwards. That the eternal Son of God should have emptied himself of his divinity when he became a man, and received it not again till this man was glorified, is an idea that can not be reconciled with the immutability of the divine nature. "If the Logos, professedly in love," remarks Dorner, "has given up his eternal, self-conscious being, where is his love during that time? Love without self-consciousness is an impossibility."* The utmost we can say is, that Christ limited himself in certain circumstances, that he did not exert his power in

---

* "Doct. of the Person of Christ," vol. iii., p. 253.

certain circumstances. All through his life we can see that there was that within him which was held back. He seemed to be under a great *redemptive law*, and beyond that law he could not go. He could have unfolded truth, which he did not unfold; could have wrought miracles, which he did not work; could have manifested power in a vast variety of ways, which he did not manifest. Christ in the sphere of Christianity acted very much as God has done in the sphere of creation and providence. God has put himself under a law of restraint. He has not revealed all that he could reveal; not done all that he could do. He has acted in the best way for the whole universe of mind. The same fact of partial repression can be seen in the inspired writings. The Bible illumines one realm of thought and being; but there is another realm which it leaves in darkness. Christ, then, acts in harmony with the whole course of the divine procedure. There is a principle of *denial* in the movements of the Redeemer; what may be called the sacrifice of negation. If we view Christ by himself, with reference to himself, this characteristic can be seen quite distinctly. He was willing, for instance, to live amidst the solitudes of the wilderness for forty days; live there in a state of hunger; not venturing to do any thing to lessen the severity of the trial. By a miracle he might provide food for five thousand persons, but not by a miracle could he provide food for himself. A principle of self-sacrifice governed him; and so the miracle-life must flow out for the benefit of man, but not for the benefit of the humbled Redeemer of man. There were times when the soul of Jesus seemed to be taxed to its utmost limit; as if redemption demanded that the whole power thereof should be exerted; as if the divine could only go so far, and then must stop; as if a full volumed agony of pain were requisite, in order to pay the redemption-price for souls. The intense mental suffering of the Saviour can not be explained, except upon the supposition that the divine was held in abeyance to a certain extent. He even said himself that God had forsaken him.

It has been a question whether Christ, *just before he expired on the cross*, received communications of divine light, enabling him to die with *gladness*, and *not* in the midst of *darkness* and *pain*. As a thought, it would be pleasant to view the Redeemer as passing away like the sun surrounded with glory; leaving the earth with a splendor the same as when first he left heaven. But however attractive such a thought might be, there is no evidence that Jesus was allowed to realize it in the last moment of his life. Not till he yielded up himself into the hands of death, was the ransom-price paid. All that was peculiarly redemptive in Christ culminated on the cross. Not till after death, therefore, was the prize to reach him; not till after death was he seen to be the Conqueror. The glorified Redeemer, and the abased Redeemer, could not meet together on Calvary.

Is it too much to say now that the redemptive consciousness of Christ was conditioned by a *law of progress?* Of course our standpoint here is strictly human. In God there is no progress. We should be inclined to think that not until a certain stage of mental development had been reached, did the idea of redemption dawn upon the soul of

Jesus. If the consciousness of the divine was gradual, the consciousness of redemption was equally gradual. And as far as the true order is concerned, the Son of man must have known that he was divine *before* he could know that he was the Redeemer; for there could be no Redeemer apart from divinity. At first we can see that Jesus was innocent; no stain upon him; pure as a star. Then habits of holiness, stronger and more fixed as the time passed, were formed in him. His life also was developed in the midst of opposition. Fierce winds struck him. He moved with a serene majesty through all contraries. Great strength and tenacity of principle were worked out. Then as his redemptive life was unusual, unusual obstacles he had to meet and overcome. The Christ of Gethsemane and the cross was greater, humanly speaking, than the Christ that lay in his mother's arms, or that stood before the doctors in the temple. He was sinless all the way through; but in degree, in compass of life, he was greater at the end: he had more *being*. At the last, when the whole ransom-price of men was paid down, the height of his development was reached. After the earthly and redemptive work was finished, we may well suppose that the human nature of Christ was most ineffably interpenetrated and surrounded with the divine; so that to speak of his development now in the eternal and heavenly places would betray a feeling of irreverence. When Christ passed out of time, he passed out of history. In the centre of the divine system he will be throned forever and ever; unfolding the glories of the Godhead to adoring and worshipping myriads; while he himself will be living in a region of existence that can not be touched or measured by the most exalted creature.

Such is the Christ of the gospels. There is this advantage in the view that has been taken, that every statement, relating to this wondrous Being in the evangelic narratives, can here find a place. None are thrown aside as improper; none are weakened or changed. Any view of Christ that can not make use of all the facts of the case is a false view. A one-sided or theoretic Christ is no Christ at all. It is evident enough that the Redeemer is every thing to men, or he is nothing. Religion rises or falls with him. The historical Christ admits of no compromise. Out of him there is no salvation. He is the centre of all Biblical teaching. Make him less than he is, and the Bible is gone; and Christianity is gone with it. We are not surprised that modern unbelief is concentrating its attack upon the person of Christ. Let him stand forth in all the royalty of his Godhead, and Christianity is safe: let him be divested of his divine claims, and Christianity is lost.

"You can never explain the enigma of primitive Christian belief, its world conquering power, and its world regenerating effects, nor the existence of the Christian Church itself, if Christ was not, and did not do, what the gospels tell of him. By trying to explain primitive Christian history as a chain of merely natural occurrences, you turn it upside down and make it an insoluble enigma. By your denial of the superhuman element in Christ, you are compelled to seek the mainspring of so immense a movement as that of Christianity in persons, circumstances, and relations, which can not bear the weight of such a superstructure;

and in the end you ask us to believe that the kingdom of truth took its origin from misunderstanding, error, self-deception, and dishonesty!"*

It is a noteworthy fact that the *holiest men* have been found among those who believed that Christ is divine. Religion has sunk the moment he was viewed as a mere creature. With the rejection of the divine in Christ, other fundamental facts have been rejected; till finally the soul has dropped down into a species of naturalism, leaving nothing but veins of morality to take the place of the religion of the Son of God. Christ is like the sun, like the air, like the heart in the human body. Take him away, and there is nothing but darkness and death.

It is not sufficient to say that Christ was a *sinless* man. If he was merely a man, and yet spoke as God, then he was a *sinful* man. His holiness never can stand along with words that we should close our ears against, if any human being were to utter them. The higher the holiness and the higher the divine claims, the more

* Dr. Christlieb's Paper before the Evangelical Alliance of 1873.

would we be startled by the two opposite characteristics. Make Christ even the noblest creature in existence; still he must be humble. The very greatness of his perfection would lead him to be all the more careful how he spoke. The purest and highest created mind would not be so likely to assume divine attributes, as a mind of lower grade. We are compelled to say that if Christ was sinless, then he was supernatural; but if not supernatural, then he was sinful. It is all in vain to attempt to hold on to the holy Jesus, and yet deny his divine claims and redemptive work. He escapes from us, and also the whole system of Christianity vanishes away, the instant we view him as the mere sinless man.

It is a significant remark of Schlegel, that "*if Christ were not more than a Socrates, then a Socrates he was not.*"* Equally striking are the words of Lessing: "If Christ is not truly God, then Mohammedanism was an undoubted improvement on the Christian religion. Mahomet, on such a supposition, would indisputably have been

---

* "Phil. of Hist," vol. ii., p. 43.

a greater man than Christ, as he would have been more veracious, more circumspect, and more zealous for the honor of God, since Christ, by his expressions, would have given dangerous occasion for idolatry; while, on the other hand, not a single expression of the kind can be laid to the charge of Mahomet."* If Christ were simply a man, having a sinless character, how is it possible for him to use language conveying the idea that he is God? He saw that the Jews understood him as claiming to be God, and that they condemned him for that reason; he saw also that Christians honored him as divine; why, then, did he not correct the mistake, if it was a mistake?

If Christ is not a theanthropic person, living a theanthropic life, there is something fearfully dark and wicked about his character. The sin of falsehood he must have carried to a complete perfection. The sin of blasphemy he must have been guilty of in a higher degree than was ever possible to any mortal man. His ambition must have gone beyond all limits. The

* Quoted in Schlegel's "Phil. of Hist.," vol. ii., p. 43.

evil he has set in motion is beyond all reckoning. He has corrupted the whole current of human history. He has deluded millions of people for nineteen centuries, and made them rank idolaters. Surely he is the great impostor of a race; a man so mighty in sin that forgiveness can not reach him. He pretends to be God, and by the very pretence sinks down to the depths of Satan. He would be worshipped, while eternal dishonor must cling to his name. He would essay to work in a supernatural sphere, above and beyond the natural laws of the universe, while he himself is the most lawless of men. He would assume to stand between God and the guilty, the only Redeemer of a fallen race, yet, by the assumption, he commits a crime for which a Redeemer can never be found. Such must be the character of Jesus, unless we view him as a divine-human Saviour.

If the necessities of the argument compel me to affirm that Christ was the great transgressor, what a mass of contradictions follow from that as matter of consequence. With one breath I say that he was the mightiest sinner of the race, while with the next breath I say that he was the holiest man that ever lived. The heart that was full of enmity communed with God! The most hateful being was loving and lovely! The most proud was the most humble! He who manifested the sweetest submission was full of unbelief! Jesus died to establish truth and righteousness, yet truth and righteousness he had none! The most depraved being founded the one religion of purity! Such is the logic; and there is no escaping from it. If it is hard to be a Christian, it is harder still to be sceptic. The unbeliever can say, "With a great price obtained I this liberty."

The only conclusion from the whole subject is, that Christ is a divine-human Saviour, and Christianity is true. No man, unless he was insane, would claim to be God and Redeemer: and if he was insane, he could not have that complete balance of character, and look of divinity, that Christ possessed. There is no other way, therefore, but to take him in the plenitude of his power and purity. Only as "God manifest in the flesh" can he be reconciled with himself.

Thou glorious Saviour! millions have given thee their heart, and made thee the joy of their soul. None have failed of thy strength who trusted in thee; none have ever grieved at the last hour who made thee their hope. Thou didst dwell in the bosom of God before time was born. In communions sweet thou didst spend the ceaseless ages. No solitude marked thy being in the timeless to-day of God. In the midst of ineffable blessedness, such as no creature can tell, thou didst move through the golden years of an infinite life. Thou camest into this dark world of sin. A stranger thou wast here. Like a divine flower brought from the lands of eternity thou didst bloom among us. Thy beauty did smile upon passing men. Thy fragrance filled the air both near and far. But rude men trampled thee down. They could not bear thy loveliness, for that reminded them of their sin; and the heavenly perfume that exhaled from thee was not to their taste. Yet the wicked could not destroy thee. During a day thou didst smile here, and at evening time thou didst bow thy head, didst lie in the dust; but on the coming morning thou wast in heaven, in the garden of God. Jesus, thou art the Holy One that came to us. Guile was not found in thy mouth, neither was the shadow of iniquity known to darken thy heart. Bad thoughts disturbed thee not. Thy emotions were like the breezes of heaven, as the ripples on the sea of the Lord, as waters of peacefulness flowing from their eternal fountains. We can not describe thee. Thou art far above us. Thou art God, and also man. We bow in thy presence. We take thee as our Saviour. Thou art our all. Forgive us our sins. Wash us in thy blood. When this frail life is ended, take us to thyself. In the kingdom that is eternal may we praise thee with love.

CHAPTER III.

SUPERNATURAL BEGINNING OF THE RELIGION OF CHRIST IN THE SOUL.

THERE is a divine remedy for sin, and that divine remedy works in a specific way. The mould of our subject is found in the very structure of the mind. As the entire soul has been affected by the fall, so the entire soul must be affected by the redemption. The mind is usually divided into three faculties: the intellect that thinks, the heart that feels, and the will that chooses. If the divine change would be complete, it must be threefold in its nature: the understanding must be enlightened, the affections quickened, the will liberated.

I. DIVINE LIGHT FOR THE INTELLECT, PRODUCING A SOUND CONSCIOUSNESS.

The difficulty with the understanding of fallen man is found in the fact that there is no spiritual apprehension to it. There may

BEGINNING OF RELIGION IN THE SOUL. 65

be correct reasoning in many things, and a real discovery of truth in many things, but, for all this, there is a sphere that is just as unknown, as colors are unknown to the blind. "The natural man receiveth not the things of the Spirit of God; for they are foolishness unto him: neither can he know them, because they are spiritually discerned." The mind needs to have a new cast and a new eye.

1. The divine light enables one to have a consciousness of *God*. It is not that the idea of God has dawned upon the mind, but it is that there is a *sense* of his existence. The impression that is made upon the soul is not from the force of argument: it is more solemn, clear, and divine than that. The creaturely spirit is in the midst of an atmosphere, and there is a realization of an Infinite Presence. The divine purity makes us to think of our sin; yet the divine love makes us to look upward with hope. Our vision becomes more clear, and the range of it more extended.

In the city hall of Brussels there is a very striking picture. On the ceiling of one of the rooms, you behold the figure of an angel blowing a trumpet. You take your stand in front of the angel, so as to gain a complete view. Having looked a sufficient length of time, you move round to the side. You are astonished, however, with the fact that there is no side! You are still standing in front of the angel, and the heavenly eyes are fastened upon you. The mind is struck with wonder; and the confession is, that this is a notable picture. You now change your position, going to what would seem to be the back part of the angel. More astonished than before, you find that there is no back part! The eye is looking straight at you. Finally, you take another point of view. It makes no difference. Go round and round that picture, and the eye follows you at every step. You stand mute and awestruck before a great presence. How much this seems like God. The Infinite Eye is ever upon us, and we are searched through and through.

2. There is a consciousness of *eternity*. It is not the mere abstract conception of time without end, but it is the profound realization of the everlasting state. When once the mind is in the mood of thinking about

eternal things, almost any thing will suggest them. The smoke that wanders away into the winter's sky; the ceaseless flow of a great river; a solitary ship beating across the ocean; a man breathing his last in the midst of hushed stillness,—each may awaken spiritual faculties, and cause souls to think of that existence that keeps on forever. No one is prepared to live until the idea of an endless destination has possessed him. The fact that men are either lost or saved in that immortal state, is a fact of infinite significance. To the serious mind the very wail of the everlasting night seems to fall upon the ear, and the music of the celestial seems to invite the spirit back to its home. A fixed thought of eternal realities reduces all things here, making mortal creatures to appear like madmen as they strive to hold fast a shadow.

3. There is a consciousness of *accountability*. It is always observable that when a person would begin the religious life his sense of accountability is sharpened. He sees duties that he has not seen before. Conscience thus takes the lead. There is before the soul a strictly *new* life. The

human spirit is musing in the midst of great moral solemnities. To act is a necessity. The only danger is that a *seemingly* right course will be chosen, instead of the one path of holiness. Men by nature are Pelagians, and they will do the work themselves if they can. The ministry of failure, however, will have its effect. The law is not as easily satisfied as was supposed. The moral consciousness is made more searching by the fact of failure, and the disappointed spirit is looking round for another way of life.

4. The consciousness of *sin* and *guilt* now characterizes the illumined soul. Sin is deeper and darker than it was wont to appear, and the feeling of guilt proportions itself to the new revelation. As to personal holiness, there is none. The man has reached the hopeful point when he can say, "I am a great sinner!" It is not to be supposed that the consciousness, whatever its compass and clearness, takes in the totality of sin and guilt. The chief point is, that the awakened spirit is in the line of true conviction. It is not so much the *intensity* of conviction, as it is the *quality* of it, that

must be looked at. There are some souls like ships that enter the harbor quite easily, and others that are swept in by a tempest. One person may have a slight sense of sin at the beginning of the divine life, and a pungent sense afterwards; while another person may have a pungent sense at the beginning, and a slight sense afterwards. The important thing is to realize that we are condemned and lost.

5. A *painful* consciousness now arises. The man has awakened out of sleep, and beholding the evils that are without and within he is troubled. A sense of misery is reasonable, because that which produces the misery is no fiction. A truthful view has been taken of great realities, and this to a guilty mind must be painful. Nothing is so fearful to a sinful soul as the *truth*. The pain is witness that things are seen, in a measure, as they are. Contentment in sin is moral insanity. To be scorched by the fires of remorse shows that there is a divine nature to the soul. We can almost imagine that an imperial mind under the full blaze of God's light would prefer to fly into the depths of perdition, rather than

make the least attempt to steal into heaven. Who can tell but that lost spirits in hell will hold themselves there by the very almightiness of conscience? It is much better to pass through the ministry of torment here, where redemption is found, than hereafter, where the reign of law and justice will have no end. "I can approve of those only who seek in tears for happiness." However quietly some souls may come to Christ, it is a question whether the absence of the painful emotions is any gain ultimately. I should suppose that a human spirit would be stronger and greater forever for having passed through agonies that proclaimed the magnitude of its sin and guilt.

6. There is a consciousness of *moral weakness*. If the human race were all philosophers, they would need the salvation of Christ to the same extent that the most ignorant men need it. By no method which the soul can adopt is there any success in the destruction of sin. The evil may be modified, but not eradicated; the rough growth trimmed, but the root of bitterness never plucked up. According to the definite Bible expression, "we are *without strength*." Most

men are even the slaves of a particular sin. With all their efforts they can not conquer it. He who is searched by the light of God feels that he is utter weakness. Despair touching self-restoration is the state of his mind. The soul longs for a way of recovery. A redemption that will arrest sin and introduce holiness is the redemption that is needed.

7. The way to be saved is now *understood*. One will never understand this way unless he is aided by the Spirit. Theological training, however valuable that may be, will never make all plain. We think of Chalmers preaching for years with no spiritual discernment touching the plan of salvation. The distinguished scholar and the little child seem to be upon the same level here: confusion marks the one about as much as the other. Indeed, it would not be strange if the child should enter the kingdom the first, leaving the scholarly man still standing at the door. The very *simplicity* of the gospel method is most puzzling to the fallen mind. The soul is either looking over the point, or away from it; trying to fasten upon something that is foreign to the case

in hand. When we sink down to nothingness and see that Christ is all, the way spreads out before us with marked distinctness. A man is never himself until he finds the Saviour.

II. DIVINE LIFE FOR THE HEART, PRODUCING SOUND EMOTION.

In the Syriac version of the New Testament we meet with the word *life*, instead of our word *salvation*. Hence certain passages read in this way: "This day has *life* come to this house." "The grace of God that giveth *life*." "How shall we escape, if we neglect so great a *life?*" Then instead of the familiar word *Saviour*, a new rendering attracts our attention: "We have heard and known that this is Christ the *Life-giver*." "This God hath raised up to be a Prince and *Life-giver*." "Our citizenship is in the heavens, whence we expect our *Life-giver*, the Lord Jesus Christ." With such a turning in language, the great fact of life from Christ stands out before us. This new power in the heart has the following characteristics.

1. There is a *holy tendency*. This holy ten-

dency of the good man is constant, just as the sinful tendency of the bad man is constant. Let the Christian look into his heart at any moment, and he will find there a pure inclination. The person is changed at the base of his being. There is in deed and in truth a "new possibility" in the soul. Yea, more, there is a divine bioplasm in the heart, and that has begun to form the new man.

2. There is a *holy taste*. Delight is found in the spiritualities of religion, which is in marked contrast with the former indifference. As the artist has a taste for art and the musician for music, so the pious man has a taste for piety. One feels at home with objects which were once centres of irritation. There is a taste for certain leading truths of the Christian system, which at one time were disliked. Excellencies connected with the Divine Being and Christ his Son are now appreciated. Spiritual beauty captivates the soul.

3. There is *holy desire* in the heart. Desire is prolonged emotion; yet the emotion is intensified and enlarged. To the extent that the soul desires to be holy, to the same extent it shrinks from sin. There is

in this way a double movement, and the double movement shows the amount of pure power. To abhor sin in its essence, and not merely in its savage dress, is the mark of a regenerate mind. The longing after holiness *per se* gives a new turn to the conscience. The moral faculty breathes a new atmosphere, and is more sensitive and tender. Kant significantly remarks, that "having a *large* conscience is the same with having *none*." He who is too great to notice what are deemed trifling sins, is a trifling sinner.

4. Divine life in the heart takes the form of *holy love*. This feeling of love bears witness to a radical change in the character, and shows wherein that change consists. There is supreme attachment to God; and that supreme attachment steadies the soul and keeps it. The thought now is to love all that is good, and to hate all that is evil. I may be asked whether one does not begin the Christian life by loving God for his *favors*, rather than by loving him with good-will and complacency? I would answer, No. If I am truly thankful to God for his favors, that presupposes that I have in my soul disinterested love; for

it is that disinterested love that gives character to the thankfulness. Mere gratitude is too narrow to form a basis for Christian character. Of course it is a fact that the infinite gift of salvation appeals most powerfully to the love of gratitude. Still that form of religion which has been started into existence by a view of the divine favors is quite certain to prove an absolute failure. Nothing but the love of moral excellence will stand.

5. We can now say that there is a *spontaneity* to all these movements of the heart. They do not have to be cajoled and flattered before they will show their power. We may come upon them suddenly and unexpectedly: they will still act according to the life that is in them. They are not the result of circumstances, ceasing to be when the circumstances are gone. In trying moments when every thing seems to be swept away, they remain. If there was no spontaneity about the inner life, one could have no confidence in his character. A religion that has to be bargained with and pressed into duty against its own inclination is not religion. If at those times when I am left

alone, with nothing finite to rest on, I can yet move straight towards Christ, then I need not fear.

What now is the connection between *second causes* and the efficient cause in the conversion of a soul? There is a very important connection. Nothing is more reasonable than to show to a fallen man the nature and magnitude of sin, the character and claims of God, the all-sufficiency of the Christian redemption, and the conditions on which it may be received. This method lays a certain dignity on the human faculties; and almost forms a channel for the new life to flow in. Although it be a fact that God is the efficient agent in changing the character of the soul, we are not to rest contented with feeble efforts on that account; but we are to strive to so illumine the mind, soften the heart, and sway the will, that it will seem as if we ourselves were wielding divine powers, and converting men. While it is true that we can not understand how it is that the Divine Spirit arrests the march of depravity in the heart, yet there are *effects* which announce his presence; and whatever may be the monitions of his love which we recognize, we must heed them. The fact that he works in the hidden solitudes of the soul should impress us with the profoundest awe, and should urge us to the attainment of 'that end which he desires so much. The air of seriousness that spreads over the mind, the sadness which tells of a nature that is crushed, the conscience that is trembling with fear, should suggest to us that God is at work, seeking to save. Silent and intent we should be; eager to catch the first sound of his footsteps; peering through the mists of the dawn; anxious for the day. Truth sounding through the soul is the voice of God; it is the pioneer of the Saviour; it is "the sword of the Spirit," cutting down evil; it is the condition by which the Divine Being limits himself.

A question now meets us of this character: Is the supernatural life which comes to souls, *confined to the people of this earth?* It is our understanding that the entire kingdom of holy creatures is animated by this life. When the angels were called into existence they had it; but those of their number that fell, lost it. When Adam was created, he was endowed with this supernatural life; but sinning, he lost it also. The race that have descended from him are by nature destitute of the life of God. By the redemption of Christ, however, we see it working again. In the act of regeneration it appears. In progressive sanctification it shows its power. When the soul is perfected, that soul will be on the same plane of existence with the sinless angel; both united to God by the supernatural life.

The person who communicates this life to the fallen and the unfallen is the Holy Spirit. Even Christ, though God-man and sinless, was nevertheless filled with the Spirit as to his human nature. This fact is striking. Why should God give "the Spirit without measure" unto him? We are accustomed to think that a divine influence is only given to *sinners;* and yet here is a person who was *holy*, receiving the Spirit with great fulness. The man Christ Jesus, I apprehend, shows to us that no creature is complete without the supernatural life. He presents to the entire universe that form of existence that may be called normal. The sinless angels, then, as well as the sinless Redeemer, must be animated by the Spirit's power. Augustine remarks, "that not only of holy men, but also of the holy angels, it can be said that 'the love of God is shed abroad in their hearts by the Holy Ghost, which is given unto them.'"* Thus instead of confining the doctrine of a supernatural life to the theology of redemption, it is rather a feature of that theology which is universal.

It would seem, however, that the supernatural life which comes to sinful men, must be somewhat different from the supernatural life which comes to sinless angels. There is opposition to battle with among men, but nothing of that kind among angels. Good must be planted in the human heart, and evil expelled. We learn from Scripture that the Spirit has to *convince* men, has to *strive* with them; and that many a time he is *grieved* because of the opposition which he meets. It is evident, then, that the grace which overcomes sinful souls must be exceedingly powerful. It not only destroys moral evil, but heals the wound which that evil has made. The supernatural life, therefore, must be *remedial* in its nature, as well

* "City of God," vol. i., p. 493.

as the spiritual element which keeps holiness in existence, and connects the creature with the Creator.

III. Divine Liberty for the Will, producing sound Action.

The sinful determination of the will includes within itself the chief part of one's character. The element of wilfulness is peculiarly the element of sin. There is nothing in which we see so much of the will as in the choice of sin. Unaided from any quarter—with the total capacity of the will—the man sins. The bad determination is absolutely a *self*-determination. In turning to God man is dependent; but in the determination to sin there is independence. We thus see a tremendous personality at work in the matter of evil. Man's guilt is in proportion to his voluntariness.

Although the soul is in bondage to sin, yet the bondage is that of choice. No one but a freeman can become a slave. The monarch has locked himself in prison, has thrown away the key, has sealed his own fate by deliberate purpose. It is not as if the soul were eager to escape from bondage, and could not. The dark and hopeless feature is, that the will is in the sin. If the voluntary faculty accepted of holiness, the fact would be apparent in a race of holy men; but inasmuch as all are sinners, it is evident that the will prefers the sin. A self-enslaved will is thus not a theory, but a fact.

Now, if a change is to take place in the character of man, that change must be chiefly in the lawless will. Unless its determination to sin is changed into a determination to holiness, there is no possibility of restoration to the image of God. A slight reform in a few individual acts does not reach the governing power. As well attempt to change the east wind by commanding a hundred men to walk against it. A person who has thoughts of a better life will sometimes put forth resolutions in the line of rectitude; thus trying to do by a promise, what he can only do by a determination of the will. There may be success in the development of outward sanctities and moralities,—the surface swept clean,—but the soul is as black and bad as ever.

In the act of liberating the captive will,

there may be great ease and peacefulness, as if the soul went into liberty with a bound of joy. There are persons, however, who have to struggle exceedingly in order to be free: it is like taking heaven by violence; like fighting for one's life. Augustine reached liberty in this way. He says: "Soul-sick was I, and tormented, accusing myself much more severely than my wont, rolling and turning me in my chain, till that were wholly broken, whereby I now was but just, but still was, held. And thou, O Lord, didst press upon me inwardly by a severe mercy, redoubling the lashes of fear and shame, lest I should again give way, and, not bursting that slight remaining tie, it should recover strength, and bind me faster. For I said within myself, 'Be it done now, be it done now'; and as I spake, I all but performed it; I all but did it; and did it not; yet sunk not back to my former state, but kept my stand hard by, and took breath. And I essayed again, and wanted somewhat less of it, and somewhat less, and all but touched, and laid hold of it; and yet came not to it, nor touched nor laid hold of it; hesitating to die to death and to live to life;

and the worse, whereto I was inured, prevailed more with me than the better whereto I was unused; and as the moment approached wherein I was to become other than I was, the greater horror did it strike into me; yet did it not strike me back, nor turned me away."*

Faith is the one act which proclaims that the will has been changed. The whole process of regeneration culminates in this great act of the soul. Faith is not single, but complex. It includes within itself the chief experiences of the soul, and makes use of the chief faculties of the soul. With my *intellect* I *see* that Christ is the divine-human Saviour; with my *heart* I am *attached* to him; with my *will* I *trust* in him. Thus *light* in the faculty of thought, *life* in the faculty of emotion, *liberty* in the faculty of action, find their developed fruit in faith. The sense of the divine, the relish for the divine, choice of the divine, mingle together, and resolve themselves into this noble grace. Perfect faith brings back the soul to its normal state. The distinguishing mark of all holy beings is, that they rest in God. The char-

---

* "Confessions," book viii., sect. xi.

acteristics of unbelief are error, alienation, and obduracy: the characteristics of faith are truth, cordiality, and willingness. The reception of Christ is always linked with penitence, while the rejection of him is always linked with impenitence. Faith is a *continuous* act. It does not begin with one moment, and end with the next. The will is set for trusting, just as the will is set for repenting. He who makes faith a mere volition, and not the steady movement of the will, is sure to have a religion that will fall to pieces when the storm strikes it. The great difficulty with the unconverted man is the fact that the will carries him along *continuously* in unbelief, impenitence, and disobedience; while with the converted man the will has a constant tendency towards faith, penitence, and obedience. Religion as it begins in the soul has value and meaning when it is viewed in this thorough manner; but make it simply a series of fragmentary acts, and it is nothing but a species of formalism.

Although we are not in the habit of thinking of actions as performed *in* the mind, there is yet a world of life in this unseen realm. The good man has his inward choices of goodness, his mental deeds of power. The soul speaks with itself, works with itself. It sounds the alarm in times of danger, encourages in times of depression, arouses in times of sluggishness, and soothes in times of trouble and grief. Sometimes a mental dialogue takes place, as if the soul were two souls; each one talking with the other, urging or restraining the other. Take also the determination of the mind to be watchful; keeping a steady look out for a day lest some great and sudden temptation should lead it off into sin. Continued watching is continued action. The soul seems to walk around the soul, all eye, all ear, lest an enemy should be found stealing in. The standing on the defensive and keeping what we have gained are to be viewed as religious acts of the mind. Positive struggles to be holy, and determined efforts put forth to overcome sin, are instances of moral action.

Let us suppose that a battle is going forward on a moonlight evening, and that the battle is reflected so as to be seen *in the clouds*. You behold men on foot charging against each other, and men on horseback flying to and fro in the air. The cannons are seen and men loading them, and the banners of different regiments float and wave in the sky. Soldiers are carrying off the wounded and the dead. Ships of war are seen also, for there is a naval conflict going forward, and men are rushing across the deck, ascending the rigging, and arranging the sails. Some of the vessels are in flames, and the officers and marines are escaping from them. In the whole movement, however, of this battle in the clouds, there is silence. The shout of the warrior is not heard, and the sound of musket or cannon falls not upon the ear. So is it with that conflict that is going forward in the soul. The will is active; but all is still: the battle is spiritual.

There is a kind of action in the mind whose shadow is faintly seen on the outside. Look at the silence of a saintly man in certain circumstances. The silence may be the result of an act of the will; it may therefore speak. The very look of the eye may be eloquence itself. It may touch the heart, may move the will, may be more powerful than human speech, more powerful than the grandest act. There may be a certain something about the man which we can not describe; yet that certain something may be full of spirituality—full of the will. The looking down or looking up, the standing still or walking a few steps, may betoken action in love of the most intense kind.

The entire Christian character, *outward* and *inward*, may be viewed as one act, including within itself vast numbers of resultant acts; just as we view the sea as one whole, with one great motion; yet having waves all over it, and these waves foaming or breaking asunder as they incline. The atmosphere that surrounds the earth is also a symbol of the active goodness of men. There is found in connection with this invisible power what may be called a motion of totality; yet along with that there are strong winds that drive ships, gentle breezes which pass over the fields, and the soft sweet air which fans the infant's cheek, and soothes the fevered brow of the dying pilgrim. Goodness, in whatever way we look at it, never sleeps. It is holy life; beating march with the heavenly times; singing always the divine psalm of love.

The divine image that was defaced, is now restored. The fire of God that went out, is now rekindled. The altar that was lost, is brought back to its place. The offering is upon it. The priestly soul is standing beside it. The temple gates that were shut, are opened. Over the gates are written these words—Here God Dwells.

CHAPTER IV.

MORALITY AND THE RELIGION OF CHRIST AS DISTINGUISHED FROM EACH OTHER.

THERE are persons who try to convince themselves that there is no essential difference between morality and religion; and as the religious man will enter heaven at last, they incline to hope that they will enter it also, the life being the same in both cases. There are others, however, who believe that the difference between morality and religion is infinite; and yet they can not tell in every particular where the difference lies. It is necessary, therefore, to present a clear statement of the two forms of life.

First, what is implied in *morality?*

1. In morality there is an idea of a *moral law.* This idea is found in all souls. We call it intuitive. It never could be the result of education, observation, or reflection. It is a ray of the Eternal Light. It

is therefore left to no man's choice whether he shall have it or not. Pleased or displeased it remains as that divine thing which can not be destroyed. No person can ever sink so low as to escape from its presence, and no one can ever rise so high as to do without its directing hand. This idea stands side by side with the idea of cause and number, of time and space. It differs, however, from these, in that it relates to that which is moral. There is such a thing as sin, and such a thing as holiness; and these retain their character forever and ever. It were as easy to make six to be nine, as to make evil to be good.

2. Another constituent of morality is a feeling of *obligation* to keep the law. Having at hand the idea of right, applying this idea to some specific duty, the soul says, Do that, you ought to do it, you sin if you refuse to do it. There is a wonderful majesty about this fact of moral obligation; a wonderful sacredness also. We seem to stand in the presence of God, and his mandate sounds through the soul. No human contrivance is the feeling of obligation. It is the workmanship of the Deity. Savage

or civilized, believer or unbeliever, each has this great feeling. Even among the idiotic and the insane we catch the echoes of a command. The sense of obligation never can be wholly destroyed. The divine never completely dies. It may be weakened and perverted, but it will speak through all eternity. It is the design of God that the feeling of obligation should be supreme. Make it secondary, and man is lost. Whether it is supreme or not, can be seen in what follows.

3. There is an attempt made *to keep* the moral law. Acts are performed that are called right; performed when hindrances are in the way; performed when a degree of self-denial is necessary. The question, however, is in regard to the intrinsic nature of the morality. Is it pure? Does it satisfy a law which can only be satisfied with holiness. Every thing has a nature. The particular nature characterizes the particular thing. The diamond, the ruby, the amethyst, are all different. Water and light, air and electricity, are not the same. Even things that resemble each other (as brass and gold) are yet entirely different. Is the

common morality of man, then, the true article? Let us see.

A person is known by the *leading drift* of his mind. Is righteousness supreme? No natural man, who knows himself, will say that it is. Morality is really the outgrowth of different kinds of feelings. A so-called moral act may be performed under the mere sense of propriety. There are men who have a fine conception of order. They want things to be done in harmony with this conception. The claims of conscience may not be any more thought of than the claims of some potentate in Asia. Consistency also may incite one to action. There are persons who have a certain moral standing in society, and to retain that standing they must act in a certain way. But consistency is not conscience, however uniform the life may be that is wrought out under its influence. A feeling of honor may also shape human action. Contempt of meanness and a love of that which is noble and generous may lead to the performance of deeds that men call great. Honor, however, is not holiness. We have known profane and drunken men who had a touch

MORALITY AND RELIGION. 93

of the honorable in their composition. The feeling of self-respect and the desire to have a good name, marshal souls into the moral line. We have also the morality of expediency. This fills out more of life than many are apt to think. Shrewd action is very often blank sin. Then we have natural compassion and sympathy as powers. Instinctive virtue, however, is not the virtue of a pure heart. If now we take the love of the agreeable—that shapes a multitude of actions. That the feeling of obligation is also acted out in a certain way, is not denied. There are persons who are quite conscientious.

Secondly, what is now implied in *religion?*

1. There is an idea of *God*. The idea is unique, just because the Being to whom it relates is unique. We think not of him as a kind of Infinite Man or Infinite Angel. In his image we are made; and yet there is that about him which never can be represented by any thing that is created. In a most significant sense he stands alone. He has no development, no dependence, no want. Then he must be viewed as existing

of necessity. The whole universe may pass away, and there be no contradiction; but an absolute Being must remain. As to the divine personality, that is wrapped up in the very idea of God. He is also apprehended as Ruler and Redeemer. To know him is eternal life. To be without God is death,—a kind of perdition.

2. There is a feeling of *union* with God through Christ. Sin is opposition to the divine character and claims, to the divine law and sovereignty; and not till the feeling of reconciliation takes the place of that opposition, is there any such thing as piety We may take the word religion from *religo*, meaning *to go back again*. As we had departed from God in the spirit of rebellion, we now go back to him in the spirit of contrite love. There is therefore friendship, and a delight in all that is divine. Unless there is delight in God and goodness, religion is impossible. "As the helianthus is said to turn towards the sun, though clouds may partially veil him, so the sincere soul will struggle towards the Light." There is a spirit of true obedience; an obedience characterized by the name godly. There is a

feeling of general good-will; such a feeling as was manifested by Christ when he came to save souls.

3. There is implied also in religion an act of *complete self-devotement* to God through Christ. Religion is not one of many good things, all as it were upon a level. It is not to be ranked with fine taste, culture, and philanthropy. Religion is not a step towards something higher, that something higher being the chief goodness. If it does not govern the soul, making servants of all the faculties of the soul, it is a delusion and dream. Religion is pure life to the spirit of man. This life warms the ideas of the reason, gives new direction to the judgment, sends health into the heart, force and freedom into the will. It is a remark of Rothe that "he only is truly pious who is so, or wishes to be so, with his whole being; not only with all his feelings and impulses, but with all the faculties of the understanding and powers of the will." The well-formed soul is not built up in separate sections, as it were by a division of labor. There is only one workman as time goes by. In fact the Christian mind is not so much a building

as a *growth*. It is like a lily rising from its germ; the one life touching all parts; the one life ending in perfection. Piety is stamped upon every thing which the pious man does. The secular becomes sacred by its touch, and the most common things become uncommon by its power. If religion is not supreme, sin is supreme. If God is not made all, self is made all.

Such is a brief statement of what is implied in morality and in religion. Each calls into play the intellect, the sensibility, and the will. There is an *idea*, a *feeling*, and an *act*, in both kinds of life. Apart, however, from this agreement, there is a marked disagreement.

Morality has not a single element which satisfies a spiritual and perfect law. The motives are not of the right character; and to keep the law is not made the great end of life. The morality is exceedingly formal and outward. Only one side of the soul seems to be in it, and that the side which can not be called spiritual. A *holy heart* moving to a holy life is not seen. The material, therefore, out of which the morality is made, is not good. And not only is it deficient in quality, but it is limited in the sphere of its action. A very few virtues will make a man moral. Let there be honesty, a degree of truthfulness, a touch of pity and benevolence, and at once the person is deemed a model in the earthly sphere. To be living without God is not thought to be a grievous offence, although it is the sin of sins. The most important duties that can belong to an immortal being are really lost sight of, and nothing but a narrow scheme of humanitarianism charms and cheats the soul.

Religion has *God* all through it. He is the beginning, middle, and end. Thus the soul takes its proper place in the divine system. There is no resting in a fair life at the very time the creaturely spirit is divorced from God. Only when in covenant with him does it live. Religion will terminate in morality, but morality can not terminate in religion. A stream can not rise higher than its source. Morality lacks vital power, because the spiritual nature is dead; it lacks authority, because the chief end is self. If I begin right, I can not end wrong; if I begin wrong, I can not end right.

The difficulty with the moral man is, that the leading sinful state of the soul has never been mastered. Every thing receives a coloring from this sinful state. Mere human morality can exist without any God at all; and just in that particular is its condemnation. A man may be a pantheist or atheist and yet be moral, as persons speak of morality. But religion can never go to any such length as that. Then, again, religion is strictly redemptive. But there is no redemption in morality. It is nothing but naturalism, or self-development. Religion, however, can have no existence apart from the supernatural. It is evident also that there is no worship in morality. When we look at those glowing descriptions of heaven which we find in the book of Revelation, we notice mingled with them ascriptions of praise like these: "They rest not day and night, saying, Holy, holy, holy, Lord God Almighty, which was, and is, and is to come." Such devotion is not possible with a dry moral experience.

But to see most truly the difference between morality and religion, I will bring forward a person who acted out these two forms of life. Take the case of Dr. William Gorden of England. He was a distinguished physician, and a man of great learning.

Let us look first at Dr. Gorden the *moralist*. "In his manners, bearing, and language, refinement and taste of the highest order were always evident. He could not do a rude, a vulgar, or an unlovely thing. Though he was abundant in his acts of private benevolence, yet he saw that far more good would be done by enabling the poor to help themselves, than by any acts of individual charity, and therefore he labored to elevate their condition intellectually and morally. In this important work he spared no pains, grudged no time, and shrank from no sacrifice. He was in a word, 'The poor man's friend.' Many hours every day were devoted to prescribing gratuitously for crowds of the indigent who frequented his house. Numerous were the cases in which he not only gave medical advice, but relieved the wants of his poor patients. It was at home, however, and amongst his intimate friends, that the loveliness of such a character could alone be fully appreciated. There his equable temper, his kindness in little things, his constant endeavor to make all around him happy, endeared him to every heart. His servants loved him as a friend, as well as respected him as a master. He gave his orders rather as if requesting a favor than issuing a command, and never suffered the least service to be rendered him, without a kind acknowledgment. In fact, humanly speaking, he seemed to be a *model man*."

We may glance now at Dr. Gorden the *Christian*. "Notwithstanding the external blamelessness of his life, he repeatedly spoke of himself, with deep emotion, as 'the chief of sinners.' He said, 'I am so *deeply* sensible of my unworthiness and wickedness! But then I look to Christ, and he has pardoned me, washed me, and clothed me in his robe of righteousness. This is why I am now contented and happy, with no dread of death, because, though I see my own vileness, I see Christ as my Saviour. *I am a mass of corruption, bat I revel in the atonement.* I can not doubt. I have been seeking religion for years by reason, but I could not get it, and I have found it by becoming a little child. I am a marvellous instance of the gracious interposition of God. If he sought me when I did not seek him, why should I doubt, now I have gone to him? Human wisdom is folly, folly! though I once did not think so. I have felt my degradation and my black wickedness, but he has forgiven me and washed me. Had I no other evidence than my own feelings, of the truth of Christianity, it would be sufficient. If all the world were anti-Christian, I should be a Christian.'"*

There is unquestionably a *sceptical* element in morality, although it is not generally perceived. If the Christian religion has any meaning, its central doctrine is the atonement of the God-man. Without this atonement, salvation is impossible. Yet the moralist affirms that his own works are sufficient. If works are sufficient, then the atonement is denied; and that, in principle, is infidelity. Again, the system of Christianity makes known to us the important fact that, unless a remedial influence is brought to bear upon the soul, holiness is not possible. The moralist, however, believes that he has a holi-

---

* Newman Hall, "Closing Scenes of the Life of William Gorden, M.D.," chap. viii.

ness of his own. If this is true, then a remedial influence coming from God is false. Christianity in this way falls to the ground. The Bible next, viewed as an inspired book, gives way; for the opinion which the moral man holds in regard to his goodness, is the opposite of what is found in Scripture. Thus morality from its nature is sceptical. The moralist should either lose all confidence in his own righteousness, and then accept of Christianity—or he should trust in his own righteousness, and then accept of infidelity. A consistent logic demands as much as this.

I think, however, that there is a class of moral men who are trying to carry forward in their minds a double movement,—they mean to be as good as they can, and hope at the same time that God in his infinite mercy will save them. They are not willing to affirm that their own works will entitle them to heaven. Their works are only a necessary part, and the divine mercy is the other part, and so with the blending of the two they hope to be saved. The system is, in a sense, natural religion. Some who adopt it are strict rationalists, and others are professed believers in Christianity. Dr. Noah

Webster inclined to this scheme of life for a time. "He placed his *chief reliance* for salvation on a *faithful discharge* of all the relative duties of life, though not to the entire exclusion of dependence on the merits of the Redeemer." "He finally, however, changed his course, feeling that salvation must be *wholly of grace.*"* The double scheme is a delusion, and is entirely contrary to the gospel system. It has in it the element of scepticism, just as morality has that element. Indeed, one is reminded by it of the deism of Lord Herbert. He depended on works and on God at the same time.

The seal of Martin Luther represented a *rose;* in the rose was a *heart*, and in the heart a *cross*. A beautiful life can only spring from pure love, and pure love can only spring from the redemption of Christ.

* Memoir prefixed to his Dictionary, pp. 21, 22.

CHAPTER V.

THE ETHICS OF CHRIST AS THEY CHARACTERIZE HIS RELIGION.

BEFORE considering the main subject, we may glance at the ethical schemes of men. The human systems can be traced back to the leading faculties of the mind.

1. That form of ethics which makes enjoyment the chief good has its home in the *sensibility*. The earliest life of the human being is passed in the midst of sensations. The child coming forth into consciousness is full of wants. The love of pleasure is the governing feeling. There is a tendency to rest in means, as if they were ends. This kind of life is often continued from childhood to manhood. There is, however, no morality in it. If I choose holiness for its own sake, I find both holiness and happiness: but if I choose happiness for its own sake, I neither find happiness nor holiness.

2. Utilitarianism considered as a philoso-

phy is the product of the *understanding*. This system demands a fine calculation of chances. A moral nature, however, does not seem to be required by it. That one class of actions are eternally right in themselves and another class eternally wrong, it does not recognize. That which is called sin in the ethics of utility can be nothing more than a mistake; and that which is called guilt can be nothing more than a feeling of uneasiness which has arisen because of the mistake. As to punishment resulting from criminality, that can find no place in the system. At the utmost there can only be suffering; suffering in order to make the man more cautious and careful in the future. If utility is goodness, then the locomotive is a very holy machine, and a man's watch a very saintly production.

3. To be enraptured with the vision of eternal beauty is that form of life which springs from the *reason*, and is deemed by a class of superior thinkers to be the ultimate life. Rising far above the material, the phenomenal, and the seeming, we are to enter the realm of pure intelligence— face to face with eternal ideas and the un-

created good. Here we find the celestial ocean that has no storms; the divine day that has no darkness. The mere activities of men in connection with business, families, and nations, are but dull movements when compared with the serene abstraction of a great spirit. There is no question but that this is an exalted life. It is not surprising that kingly minds have been attracted towards it. It seems to ease the wandering spirit of its grief; carrying it away to a region that has no pain. Strictly speaking, however, it is neither morality nor religion. It is simply a transcendental form of life. Wisdom is made the true virtue; the abstract philosopher the true saint.

4. We come now to the ethics of *conscience*. There is a moral quality in actions. Duty is the chief thing. With my intellect I affirm that a statement is true or false: with my conscience I affirm that an action is sinful or holy. Is the life of duty the complete life? No. A man may pay a debt because it is right; pray to God because it is right; and yet he may not want to do the one or the other. This shows that unless the feelings are holy,

nothing is holy. A just man may be a bad man.

5. Another theory makes the ethical life to start from the *will*. The will is not merely the sign of personality; it is viewed as personality itself. All goodness, therefore, must centre in it. To be good is to have a good will: to be bad is to have a bad will. "There is nothing in the world," says Kant, "which can be termed absolutely and altogether good, a good will alone excepted." "A good will is esteemed to be so, not by the effects which it produces, nor by its fitness for accomplishing any given end, but by its mere good volition, that is, it is good in itself."* Most assuredly this is not a selfish theory. No man by nature, however, has such a good will; and no man by nature can tell us how to make the will good.

Every theory mentioned fails, because man himself is a failure. Sin as a fixed state of the soul is entirely forgotten. The deaf are simply trying to make known to us the philosophy of hearing. In the ethics of Christ we see a difference. They view us

* "Metaphysic of Ethics," pp. 1, 2.

as we are, and lead us out to what we should be. Divine aid comes to the despairing soul. There must be a power beyond truth and the highest ethics, or man is doomed forever. Christ puts especial emphasis upon the *heart*, and especial emphasis upon the *Spirit* who changes it. It is not possible to live a holy life without a holy heart. The distinguishing mark of Christian ethics is, that they do not simply tell us that we must have the spirit of obedience in order to please God, but they tell us how that spirit of obedience can be found. We thus begin right, and must end right.

Since Christ is a new character in history, sustaining a new relation to the whole of mankind, it is evident that a complete system of ethics must mention a *class of duties* which we *owe to such an exalted person*. If these duties should appear singular and exceptional, to the extent that no mere creature can exact them of us—that will only be an evidence of their soundness, inasmuch as they point to One who has a right to be honored and obeyed. If a remarkable virtue called faith is made fundamental in the ethics of Christ, that only proclaims the fact that there is a Saviour who must be trusted if we would reach holiness and God; and if this deepens the sinfulness of man, it only furnishes another argument for the perfection of the gospel morality. In every scheme of human ethics, there is a deficiency at some point; but in the ethics of Jesus not the least flaw is perceptible. To speak of the errors of Christ's teaching, is just as fruitless as to speak of the sins of his life.

According to Christian ethics the central power is *love*. This shows that we have entered an entirely new realm. There is energy, freshness, warmth. We are to love God with all the heart, soul, mind, and strength. One of the saddest signs of the lapse of men is the fact that God is left out of their ethical schemes. "Whatever other benevolence or generosity towards mankind, and other virtues, or moral qualifications which go by that name, any are possessed of, that are not attended with a *love to God* which is altogether above them, and to which they are subordinate, and on which they are dependent, there is nothing of the nature of true virtue or religion in them.—

And it may be asserted in general that nothing is of the nature of true virtue in which God is not the *first* and last."*

Another characteristic, however, of Christian ethics is the striking fact that we are called upon to *love Christ supremely.* With the utmost distinctness he says: "He that loveth father or mother more than me is not worthy of me." This is certainly a new kind of ethics; new in their object and new in their nature. The fact that Christ is God-man and Redeemer, makes it perfectly safe to fix the heart upon him with supreme attachment. All throughout the New Testament, Christian action is made to revolve around the Saviour of men. Are we to forgive? "God for Christ's sake hath forgiven us." Must we be willing to suffer? "Christ suffered for us, leaving us an example that we should follow his steps." Are we exhorted to walk in love? "Christ also hath loved us, and hath given himself for us." Are we to assist those in want? "The Lord Jesus Christ for our sakes became poor." Must we pray? "If ye ask any thing in my name, I will do it." Do we

---

* President Edward's "Works," vol. ii., p. 271.

wish to catch hold of the ultimate motive?
"The love of Christ constraineth us."

Glorious love! How inimitable is thy beauty! Thou standest alone among the stars of God. Thy day has no night; the sky that surrounds thee no cloud. Thou art the only true expression of the Deity. What is expediency beside thee? What is pleasure? Yea, what is duty itself? Thou art able to perform deeds and conquer hearts where duty fails. Right is thy companion, and ever shall be; yet thou art nearer to us than right. Order and law thou knowest. Thou seemest to be both of these, and better than both. Heaven is about thee. Thy benedictions fall upon our ear; sweeter to us than the seraphim's song. Thy presence shall be to us hope; and joy shall gladden our path because thou art near. Let thy healing power fill every channel of our being; so that we shall breathe with comfort as the hours pass; crippled not again by the raging power of sin. May we have meditations of sweetest life, such as the royal people have upon the hills of God. Thou Messenger of goodness, how much we need thee! Many a time we are laid low.

With firm steps and sure may we walk the ways of life; thou going with us till the end is reached; granting us courage when we are inclined to sink, and strength to bear up in the storm. Leave us not till every stain is taken away and every wound healed; love enthroned in the heart, and the sabbath of heaven abiding with us forever.

Christian ethics look with special favor upon the grace of *humility*. As humiliation characterizes the entire life of Christ, so humility should characterize the entire life of the Christian. Aristotle calls attention to "the noble-minded" and "the little-minded," but it does not appear that either of these characters possessed that virtue which we call by the name of humility. Indeed, in pagan ethics, this lovely trait would be viewed as a blemish, rather than as a virtue. It is a universal truth, however, that goodness is impossible unless it springs from an humble state of heart. The fact is worthy of notice that poverty of spirit is the first beatitude which Christ mentions in his Sermon on the Mount. He thus struck at pride, and made the sense of nothingness the basis and beginning of a holy life. It is reported of St. Elizabeth of Hungary that, on a certain time, beholding the image of the dying Saviour, she took off her crown. Being blamed by her mother-in-law for this act, she replied: "Dear lady, do not blame me; behold before my eyes the sweet and merciful Jesus crowned with thorns, and can I, who am but a vile creature, remain before him wearing pearls, gold, and jewels? My coronet would be a mocking to his thorny wreath."* This shows a fine spirit. "Humility is like the eye which sees every thing but itself." If love is the fulfilling of the law, humility is the fulfilling of love. Pride shut the gate of heaven: humility opens it. The idea of *merit* which runs through all human systems of ethics and religion, is not recognized in the ethics and religion of Christ. The fact that we are justified by faith, and not by works, compels us to look for merit in the redemptive righteousness of the Son of God. The ethics of Jesus are thus entirely unique. They stand just as much alone, as he stands alone in the history of man.

Although we do not have a *system* of

---

* Montalembert's "Life of St. Elizabeth," p. 124.

Christian ethics, the *principles* are of such a nature that they reach out to whatever is essential. Dr. Temple, however, informs us that "it is in the history of Rome, rather than in the Bible, that we find our models and precepts of political duty, and especially the duty of patriotism."* The inference would be from this statement, that Christians are not sufficiently possessed with the virtue of patriotism; that the Bible being deficient in this one particular, those who believe in it are equally deficient. Is it not a fact, however, plainly seen in the past, that religious men are the most faithful defenders of their country? It can not be denied that the Roman patriotism had a large infusion of vain-glory mixed up with it; and the very people who were deemed the greatest became the lowest: the passion that was in them devoured itself and died. The Christian patriotism has a grounding of liberty and justice, love and the glory of God. The truth is, a sound character is the soul and inspiration of all that is good. The Christian is from his nature a law to himself in whatever sphere he may be placed. He

* "Essays and Reviews," p. 20. English ed.

does not need to read over the whole system of jurisprudence in order to be a good citizen. He is a good citizen because he is a good man. Let all the statutes of the land be abolished, and he would still be faithful. The character that can not hold together unless it has rules and specifications for every thing, is a very imperfect character. True enough the Bible does not present us with an elaborated system of ethics. It knew better than do that. It plants great principles in the heart,—and speedily the good father, neighbor, and citizen appear on the stage of life. Whatever may be the culture and civilization of any period, the Christian ethics are sure to match that period. Their adaptedness to all circumstances is one mark of their divinity. Instead of coming short of the highest human development, they will always go beyond that development. They know nothing of any new virtue. Neither in theory nor practice can such a virtue be pointed out.

The gospel narratives present us with moral perfection in a *person*, and not as a mere abstract ideal. Plato tried to form the conception of a perfect man, just as he tried to form the conception of a perfect republic, yet neither the man nor the republic has ever been seen. There remains nothing but the cold silent thought, looking upon us as the star looks upon us in the darkness. Neander, speaking of the "Relation of the Grecian to Christian Ethics," says: "We see in the Stoical ethics the necessity not merely of thinking of morality in an abstract general way, but of presenting a picture of moral conduct stamped in clear, individual features. Such a picture the idea of the *sage* should furnish. The sage in the empirical manifestation, exhibits himself as aiming, in his efforts, at the ideal. But he who is conceived of as endeavoring to reach the ideal, involuntarily confounds himself with his ideal, and this leads to the sage's *self-exaltation* to the *deifying of human nature*."* Thus there was a failure. The very height to which the sage seemed to go only intoxicated him; and so he fell in his attempts to rise. Better for us that we can behold moral perfection in a person; moral perfection acted out during a lifetime; acted out in the very same circumstances in which we

---

* "Bibliotheca Sacra," vol. x., p. 491.

are placed. The fact is patent to us; we are impressed by it; holier we become on account of it. Give to us the Redeemer, and at once we have a perfect system of morals. Christian ethics are simply the expression of Christ's life. We go back, then, to the fountain-head. The Perfect Exampler is before us. A power comes to us from the living Christ, more inspiring than from his ethical system, though the one is the counterpart of the other. A law or an ideal never can lift us as a person can.

There is no telling to what an extent Christ has influenced the spirits of men. He has touched all modern life. Even the most wayward heart feels his power. The wisdom of many a sceptic is his light, and the virtue of many a moralist has come from him. The very strength by which men destroy the temple of God is not their own, and the weapons with which they contend are the spoils of Calvary and the cross. There is a spiritual atmosphere all around us that he has created, and we breathe that when we know it not. None of us are the same that we would have been had he not appeared. In some way or another he has blessed us all. The very child seems to be different because he has lived, and the way through death is not so dark because he has passed through it. Perhaps the wicked are more desperate because they have grieved his love, while the saintly are more Godlike because they have found a home in his heart. In the ages of the future he will be more powerful than in the ages of the past. A wider realm he will fill, and a loftier race he will fit for heaven. In the slow marching years the world shall at length bow before him, and the Man of Nazareth and the Son of eternity shall be king over them all.

Our sense of obligation is greatly deepened by the ethics of Christ. Exceedingly important truth is condensed, and pressed upon us. We seem to have come into contact with normal forces. The divine law with its compass of requirement, pure spirituality, mighty sanctions, awes the soul, and arouses it to action. The simple fact that we are sifted and searched, makes us to see how much of evil clings to us. A rounded thought of the holiness of God startles us. A vision of the purity of Christ extends the area of our obligation. One single duty, in which are seemingly wrapped up all other duties, may so bring us to a stand that the weight of worlds will press upon us. Just to the extent that any mind feels its accountability, just to that extent is its worth and greatness seen. It is not mere knowledge that makes the man, but it is moral power, great moral action. Christ himself has presented to us a picture of obligation when he had to carry the burden of a world's guilt. The spiritual nature is to keep widening and deepening till the whole weight of responsibility that comes from a perfect law shall rest upon us, and we shall carry it with love.

As the ethics of Christ run into the plan of redemption, motives to faithfulness are multiplied. We discover a new way of looking at the universe; a way that expresses the actual state of things. This actual state of things appeals to us with unwonted power. Facts and laws, principles and persons, move our soul. Throughout the New Testament, we meet with such motives as "the mercies of God," "the unsearchable riches of Christ," "the love of the Spirit," "the powers of the world to come." Every fair-minded person must admit that the Christian life is a new form of life. There are sceptics who tell us that the ethics of Buddhism and the ethics of Christianity are about equal in value; and that it makes no great difference whether a man is a Christian or a Buddhist. Now, while some of the principles may appear to be the same in both systems, it is evident that the character which is formed by Christianity differs in *kind*, and not merely in degree, from that which is formed by Buddhism. A veritable Christian is altogether a new type of man.

Christian ethics are essentially the *ideal* ethics of the universe. If we are to love God with all the powers of the mind, and our neighbor as ourselves, that must be the rule for every intelligent being throughout the system of the Creator. The angels in heaven can do nothing more than this: Adam in Paradise could do nothing more. Even when we reach out to the Divine Being and test his character, we can find no better statement than the Bible one—"God is love." The law of love admits of no sin; it therefore contains all goodness. Let it be carried out, and the whole world would be holy and happy. Supposing that the human race had never sinned, no other law could have governed them but the law of love. The ultimate standard, therefore, is reached.

CHAPTER VI.

WORSHIP AS A CENTRAL FEATURE OF THE RELIGION OF CHRIST.

THE word "worship" is composed of *worth* and *ship*. On the one hand, God is *worthy* of honor because he is God; and on the other hand, the worship which we render to him must have *worthiness*. If it has not this quality it is *worthless*, and not worship.

The *simplicity* of Christian worship arrests attention. A religion that is false, is usually intricate. When Christianity became corrupt, it became burdensome in its forms of worship. The only two rites which characterize the religion of Jesus are noted for their simple beauty. By the aid of water, typical of purity, we are set apart to the service of the triune God. By the aid of bread and wine, symbolizing the death of Christ, we are led to think of the incarnate Redeemer. No elaborate system meets us. No gorgeous ritual absorbs the affections, and keeps the mind away from God. We behold no altar, no sacrifice, no priest, no temple. Each heart is an altar, each soul a sacrifice, each Christian a priest, each mind a temple. The Christian worship comes out of the soul, and not out of symbols. There is no rigid drill by the aid of manifold ordinances. "The simple and unimposing character of the Christian ritual," says Dr. Caird, "is an indication of spiritual advancement, inasmuch as it arises from the fact, that while the rites of Judaism were mainly *disciplinary*, those of Christianity are *spontaneous* and *expressive*. In the old dispensation, ritual observances constituted an elaborate mechanism for the awakening of religious thought and feeling; in the new economy, they are the actual and voluntary manifestation of religious thought and feeling already existing." "Besides this, the gospel rites are *commemorative*, whilst those of the former dispensation were *anticipative*. To depict the unknown, a much more elaborate representation is needed than merely to recall the known. To reproduce in the mind the idea of a former friend, is a simpler and easier process than to portray the aspect and character of a stranger."* Christianity being the final religion, it is fixed, clear, and unmaterial. The shadow is lost in the substance.

As a necessary condition of worship, there must be a *vivid conception of God*. A dull and distant thought of Deity will not answer. The mind must be aroused and vitalized. It must be in a frame in which it can think and feel and act with reference to God. Emotion must be in the will and intellect, as well as in the heart. The soul must be *possessed* as it were with God. Men are possessed with thoughts of power, of ambition, of fame, of learning, of wealth, and of pleasure. Many are possessed with a domineering appetite, with passions that can not be conquered, with a heavy indifference, with a sharp opposition to the pure and the divine. Some are possessed with the supremacy of reason, as if they were gods —worshipping themselves. Others are possessed with ideas of mystery, and with contradictions which they find in the kingdoms of nature and life. They adopt the religion of despair. The Christian must be possessed

* "Sermons," pp. 340, 344.

with that which is divine. He must have the true *enthusiasm,*—being in God.

If a man is to think at any time, he must think when he approaches God in worship. Any thing like haste or rashness is unsuitable. The preparation for coming into the divine presence is *thought;* careful and discriminating thought. Our ideas touching the Most High must be lengthened and rounded, until he stands before us as the Great Reality. To the extent that it is possible, *God* is to impress us. There is to be such a conception of his nature, character, plans, and works, that we shall be filled and arrested by the wonderful thought. No doubt a single phase of the Infinite Being, pondered carefully, will awaken intense emotion; but yet, for the sake of health and safety to the soul, our views of the Godhead must have compass. We are sure to be one-sided in our character, if our views of God are one-sided. Although we can not grasp the Infinite, we must none the less have a certain measured order when we think about the Infinite. If I am simply captivated with his power, his wisdom, or his will, I am sure to be unhinged and unbalanced. Or if I think of him as the immutable God, the sovereign of law, justice, and order, and go no further than these, I am locked up as in a prison. Or again, if his love attracts me, and I lose sight of all else but that, I am bewildered by a divine brilliancy, till finally I behold nothing with distinctness. There is no other way than to take God as he is. Any soul that will do this, will be enriched. There will be a certain majesty and divinity about the mind, just because the divine thoughts are allowed to fashion it. When one thus situated attempts to worship his Maker, we can see that there is a finished intelligence at work. The Object to be worshipped is realized. There is no blind homage. All is suitable in the given circumstances. The soul is therefore blessed, and God is glorified.

As a vivid conception of the Divine Being is all-important in the matter of worship, *preaching* comes in as tending to produce the state of mind that is wanted. Strictly speaking, preaching is not worship. It is simply an aid to worship. Both the preacher's and hearer's mind may be brought into a worshipping state by the thoughts of the sermon. Worship may even be ascending to God at the very time one is listening to the truth. Preaching and worship may thus blend together; as if preaching at its highest altitude were a species of worship. I think it is evident at any rate, that the action of the mind upon the truth, or the truth upon the mind, is the proper antecedent of worship. One must either be in a meditative state by himself, or he must be in that state while listening to the utterances of the preacher.

The proclamation of divine truth is a most reasonable method of impressing the mind. This presupposes, however, that the preaching has *weight*. A certain reverence must be paid to the higher faculties of the mind. The soul is not merely immortal itself, but it has a great deal in it that is equally immortal. Then it links itself on to God, and its destiny is never to be separated from him. How fit, then, that it should be treated in a way that harmonizes with this exalted state. If it is the command of Scripture to "honor all men," most assuredly the soul should be honored by presenting to it great thoughts. These thoughts are to be cast in the mould of argument, inasmuch as man is a reasonable being. The mind will reason, whether it be truly or falsely. There is a logic which all men have; and sooner or later they will face the great problems of life. A discourse that will command the attention of the soul, must have power and system. It must betoken labor. The life-blood of the emotions must be in it. The wondrous themes of Christianity are to be presented in a dress that is suitable to their exalted character. Style and thought are to go together. The common-place is out of place. Truths are to come to us in their own fulness; clear as their own eternal light; vital with that life that appertains to God. Their strength will make the soul to be strong, and kingly with all the majesty of truth. There is to be warmth, but not that of mere excitement. The heat is to come from the fires of God: pure, powerful, permeating the whole being, making the soul to worship as if in the temple of heaven.

A thoughtful reading of Scripture is also a concomitant of worship. A sense of the divine should go with us as we scan the sacred pages. If the sermon should cause us to have a vivid conception of God, the

Bible should heighten that conception. We are now face to face with the Supreme Author himself. We are reading the very words of God. The thoughts of God are moving through our soul. Impressions are made upon us which are never made by any other means. We see truth in a new light, it holds us by a new authority, it stamps a new image upon the soul. A single passage from the Bible will sound the depths of the human spirit, as not even the finest passage from the writings of man can attempt to do. There is a certain frailty about all human thoughts. They are struck with the disease that affects sinful souls. The utterances of God are life. They carry on their countenance the bloom of health. They speak with power to the strongest men. There is a certain *massiveness* about the leading Biblical statements. There is nothing of the empty or the forced. We catch the idea of silent power and divinity. The mind is rendered serious. It is set in an attitude for worship. Then there is an under-current of pathos running through many parts of the divine writings. There is nothing worked up as if it were made to order.

There is simply the natural flow of pensive emotion, stealing out as it were in secret. Its very fineness and spirituality cause it to enter the soul without a witnessing eye. One feels in a certain mood without knowing how he came into it. The soul is prepared for worship as if angels had been working with it, or as if seraphs had breathed upon the heart while they passed by on their way to God. "It may be said of the Bible," remarks Henry Rogers, "that it has made susceptible of pathos, and brought within the range of human emotion, subjects which had hitherto dwelt in the region of remote abstractions, or, if they ever came nearer, came in forms which awakened only awe or terror. To familiarize, to endear, the thought of God, without degrading the conception; to bring him within the sphere of human affections, without impairing his majesty, is the triumph of the Bible."* The devotional mind is the result of meditation on Scripture thoughts. There are many parts of the Bible that seem almost themselves to be worship; as if they were clothed with form and were adoring God; their chantings

---

* "Superhuman Origin of the Bible," p. 295.

falling upon the ear like the voices of penitent men, and their melody sweet as that which comes from the choirs of the Lord. There are passages in the gospels and the epistles, in the book of Revelation and the Psalms, that lead us at once into the great temple of the Almighty; as if we were standing among the companies of the celestial during the morning worship of heaven; praising the Highest One in the midst of peace, and gladness that has no pain.

It is the peculiarity of worship upon earth that it is *redemptive*. The worship of unfallen beings has no redemptive features. It is worship in all its sanctity and singleness; centering not in a person called the Redeemer. The worship of man is entirely different from this. It can not begin or continue except through the power of Christ; can not reach God except through the divine-human Saviour. The Redeemer is every thing. The worship, however, is not merely inspired by Christ; does not merely pass through him to God: Christ himself is worshipped. He being the Eternal "Word who was with God, and who is God," we adore him. Not to do this would be to set aside the plan of redemption, would be to reject the Divine Being himself. "Whosoever denieth the Son, the same hath not the Father." The worship that finds its heart and home in the suffering Saviour, has elements and thoughts which give it a superior value. The Christian has new experiences of God's love and mercy, which the sinless angels have not; and so his worship has a uniqueness on that account. When the worship of saintly men is absolutely pure, as it will be in heaven, it will have a richness and sublimity which never can be equalled by the worship of unfallen spirits. As the incarnation and redemption of the eternal Son of God are the most notable wonders that are to be found in the universe, so the life and worship that spring from them must be superlative in their nature.

When I analyze the Christian emotions, I see at once that they find their proper outlet in worship. As Vinet truly remarks, "Worship is the purely religious form of religion. It is adoration in act." "A rite is a metaphor in action, while worship is action itself." * I no sooner think of God,

* "Pastoral Theology," pp. 178, 179.

and of man, and of the Mediator between God and man, than I think of worship. I am solemnized by a sense of the divine presence. I reverence the Divine Being. I worship him. As I look at the leading emotions of my heart, I find them all to be prayers. When I *sigh* as I think of life and of death, of worlds unknown and infinite time, that sigh is a prayer. The *penitence* which I exercise is not the penitence of a moment or an hour; it is in fact the ceaseless cry for pardon. Am I *thankful* that Mercy has smiled upon me? The thankfulness is of the very essence of worship. Do I *desire* to reach moral perfection? That desire is a prayer. Do I *love* the Absolute Loveliness? That seems like silent worship. Am I *hoping* to reach heaven through the blood of the Lamb? That is a kind of half-formed supplication. Does a feeling of *admiration* arise in my soul as I think upon the works, providence, and perfections of God? The admiration is one of the leading phases of worship. Thus the governing emotions of the Christian mind, present us with the rudiments of worship. These emotions are the pulsations of the inner life, the breathings after God, the perpetual incense that ascends on high, the sacrifice that finds acceptance with the Holy One. Without these hallowed movements of the regenerate heart, worship would be impossible.

Real prayer, however, is not mere feeling; it is the *expression* of feeling. The desires of the soul are incarnated in language, and with the language I address God. Thus the subjective and the objective join themselves together. I feel my sin, and *ask* for pardon. I feel my weakness, and *ask* for strength. All prayer is *distinct*. There is always an object in view. The cloudy or the indefinite finds no place in supplication. Prayer is no reverie, no mystic speech, no pious meditation, no descanting on the works and ways of God. Prayer should have point. It should go direct to heaven, telling what it wants. I make no speech, address no man when I pray. The attempt to be eloquent, the attempt to make a great prayer, is not prayer. The Divine Being only is before me. I think of him. I pray to him as my heart leads. If I want truth to prevail, evils to cease, souls to be saved, I pray for these things. If my faith is weak, my hope dim, my love cold, I pray that the faith may be stronger, the hope brighter, and the love warmer. If I feel grateful to God, I express my gratitude. If his greatness and glory thrill my soul, I adore him. If creaturely objects captivate me, I pray that my heart may be set on God. If I can not see my way, I pray for light. Thus all is definite. I do not wander from object to object, not knowing very well what I am doing; trying it may be to make a prayer, but not praying.

Sometimes the soul labors in its emotion. There is mental pain. The desire is heavy. It is oppressive. There is a kind of agony. One feeling swallows up all the other feelings. It is difficult to find language by which to express the burdensome emotion. There is a tendency, therefore, to hold on to a sentence, and to repeat it, when it seems to echo forth the great feeling of the soul. When Christ was in an agony, there was a divine condensation about his words; and his prayer was repeated. He could simply say: "O my Father, if it be possible, let this cup pass from me: nervertheless, not as I will, but as thou wilt." "The second time he prayed, saying, O my Father, if this cup may not pass away from me, except I drink it, thy will be done." "He prayed the third time, saying the same words." This is the way the soul acts when swayed by powerful emotions. There is unity also to the mind by reason of the singleness and power of the feeling. The prayer from the nature of the case is short. Or if it is lengthened, it will have a number of similar expressions. The urgent prayers of the Bible are of this character. In the book of Daniel we have such language as this: "O Lord, hear; O Lord, forgive; O Lord, hearken and do; defer not, for thine own sake, O my God." This is the language of earnest, painful emotion. It expresses itself in broken sentences.

When we approach God in prayer, there is a suitable balancing of *awe* and *freedom*. On the one hand, we do not rush into the divine presence; and on the other hand, we do not fear to pronounce the infinite name. The great Augustine, though he carried with him a profound sense of sin and guilt, had a holy freedom and boldness when he approached the Divine Being. "Indeed, the feeling which Augustine bears towards the Blessed Triune God, can not be better expressed than by the word *affectionateness*. There is in his experience awe 'deep as the centre'; there is humility absolute; there is the reverential fear of the wing-veiled seraphim; but there is, also, in and through it all, that confiding love which is both warranted and elicited by the dying prayer of the Redeemer."* The Moravians have been distinguished for their ease and childlike freedom in the whole of their worship. This characteristic has been cultivated by a vivid sense of Christ as their *God* and *Saviour*. He seems to be so near to them, that they open their heart with gladness. They have a present salvation, a present Saviour, and so with an assured faith and a fervent love they offer up their supplications. The primitive Christians were very much in the same blessed state. They thought of Christ, loved him, worshipped him. They were not servants, but friends. The more the Christly

---

* Prof. Shedd's Introduction to "Augustine's Confessions," p. 19.

element enters into our piety and our prayers, the more shall we have a suitable balancing of awe and freedom.

We come now to the fact of *praise* as a constituent of worship. The soul is charmed by a conception of the divine glory, and so it praises the Divine Being. When we turn to the Psalms, we are struck with the flow of exultant emotion. We hear David saying: "I will extol thee, my God, O King, and I will bless thy name for ever and ever." "I will speak of the glorious honor of thy majesty, and of thy wondrous works." "Praise the Lord with harp: sing unto him with the psaltery and an instrument of ten strings." We notice here a certain exuberance and joy. The flood gates of the soul are opened, and the glad feelings of praise rush forth. There is a degree of ecstasy; a species of holy abandon. Perhaps the Oriental mind was emotional and expressive. Western natures are colder; not so easily moved; not inclined to sound forth gladsome feelings. Still our praise should have vitality and volume. There should be tone to it. Heart is needed, whether the worship is ecstatic or calm.

Our hymnology is not always fitted for

praise. There are hymns which are hortatory in their nature. They make us to think of preaching; and when sung, they are rather aids to worship, than worship itself. Take this hymn as an instance:

> "Come, ye sinners! heavy laden,
> Lost and ruined by the fall,—
> If you wait till you are better,
> You will never come at all:
> Sinners only,
> Christ, the Saviour, came to call."

It is perfectly proper to sing hymns of this character, just as it is proper to preach the truth of God. The gospel can be sung as well as preached. It should be known, however, that to sing such hymns is not strictly worship. There are other hymns which are of the nature of a meditation. Take this one as a specimen:

> "When musing sorrow weeps the past,
> And mourns the present pain,
> How sweet to think of peace at last,
> And feel that death is gain!"

There would not be much reason in saying, "Let us worship God, in singing the above hymn." As a thoughtful piece of poetry it may answer; but not as the channel or expression of worship. The sentiment of many hymns, however, is that of direct praise. These for example:

> "Jesus, lover of my soul."
> "Rock of ages cleft for me."
> "Great God! how infinite art thou!"
> "Praise to thee, thou great Creator!"

The adoration of God in psalms and hymns and spiritual songs is to be a fact. Nothing is to be substituted for this. However eager we may be to impress the souls of men, the full-volumed worship of God is to be made the chief matter. Worship is an *end;* not the means to an end. If I attempt to worship God as a means of spiritual improvement, I do not worship him at all. Professor Schöberlein, in his "Theory of Public Worship," states the point in this way: "Even the object of edification, itself the purest and most comprehensive that could have been contemplated, did not originate worship. Do I pray, praise God, and give thanks, *in order* to edify myself? Such express design throws the soul into a position and state injurious to the simple, childlike feeling of worship, and so hinders real edification. *Design* and *effect* should not be confounded in this matter. An *effect* of worship is indeed the *good* of the soul, just as the divine pleasure is also. But, exactly when we *do not seek these as objects*, are they the most certain to follow." *

Praise to God naturally connects itself with *music*. This is finer and more ethereal than human speech. It is really a language by itself. It sounds the depths of the soul as no words of man can ever sound them. It can awaken fear and terror, sublimity and wonder, joy and sadness, hope and courage, love and hatred. It seems to work its way through the human spirit as if it were a divine essence. It starts a class of emotions that are somewhat indefinite, and very powerful just because they are indefinite. Those cries of the soul that speak to the ear of God, the longings that go out to unbounded realities, the hidden fires that seem to burn forever, are all touched and moved by the power of music. We are awed into silence, or hurried forward into the most impetuous action, by its mysterious influence. It melts many a heart that is hard, and causes day to shine upon the soul

* Presbyterian "Quarterly Review," vol. vi., p. 426.

that is wrapped in gloom. We think of music as if it were a kind of heavenly language; as if the angels used it during their day of love; and glorified men praised God with it in the courts of life. That music is a fit vehicle for worship can not be doubted. It gives expression to all the feelings. The devotional mind is at home where it is found. Praise languishes where it is not known.

"In all Christian worship," says Julius Müller, " an exalted place must be given to music. It is distinguished from sculpture, and painting, and architecture, by its capability of repetition; its capability of most diversified uses, as a representation of a great variety of objects, and in forms and conditions not less numerous. In the other arts, we have presented before us but a single object or a single group of objects, in one fixed and unchangeable attitude; a representation of but one condition, and one phase of feeling. The idea of succession, of movement, of activity, is foreign to these arts; while in music there may be endless variety. Hence is music capable of entering into the province of worship with such liveliness, and such strength of effect. A musical composition is capable of becoming, as it were, a history of the interior life of man, of his separation from God, of his fellowship with Christ."*

The very fact, however, that music is such a power, may lead one to fix the mind upon it as the chief thing; and thus worship be gone altogether. The sweet sounds attract; the music is a good in itself; the soul, therefore, rests in it. Formalism in this way is introduced; introduced almost unconsciously. It is to be feared that the department of praise in public worship is, in many cases, nothing but a mere name. The hearts of the professed worshippers do not ascend to God in the language of the hymn, aided by the music. They sing; sing with sweetness and life; but not with the spirit and the understanding. Praise must assume its rightful place in the Christian mind. The idolatry of form must give way to the pure worship of God.

* "Bibliotheca Sacra," vol. xiv., p. 814.

CHAPTER VII.

DECAY IN THE RELIGION OF CHRIST FROM CAUSES IN HUMAN NATURE.

VIEWING Christianity ideally it has no principle of decay. Like its Author it is complete. But viewing it as a life in fallen souls, struggling to restore them to the image of God, it works under great disadvantages. That there are Christian men who battle most nobly with inward corruption, and who show scarcely any symptom of moral decline, is a pleasant fact; but there are others who yield to the tendencies of a bad nature. "If you make a dog a king, will he not still gnaw leather?"

I. DECAY IN RELIGION FROM EVILS OF THE HEART.

1. Decay from indifference. A heart that is partly sanctified, is a heart that is partly stupefied. Indwelling sin is indwelling death. Every Christian is conscious of a certain dull-

ness; and if he yields to that he sinks. "The Scythians used to strike the cords of their bows at their feasts to remind themselves of danger." If we are intent against heaviness it will flee away.

2. Decay in religion may spring from the love of ease. Love of ease is the twin-sister of indifference. It wishes neither to carry a cross nor to walk through darkness. The great responsibilities, the severe duties, the self-denials of the Christian calling, it wants not. The love of ease is pure indolence and selfishness. He who listens to this feeling loses power. He does nothing, and is nothing. There are birds that pass on to the sunny south through storms as well as through pleasant skies, while others rest on their way till the mists and clouds depart. If we would win we must work. Great hindrances may be great helps.

3. A careless habit will open the way to spiritual declension. He who forgets his Bible, his closet, his church, is in the arms of death. Forgetfulness is one of the broad ways of sin. A ship can be lost by carelessness as well as by design. The evils of life come mainly through inattention. If I

mind not I find not. Many a Christian lands himself in darkness, because he thought not of the light. Souls are lost at no cost. "Every man has a weak side; but a wise man knows where it is, and will be sure to keep a double guard there."

4. The attractive element of sin may draw the mind away from the path of holiness. The fallen nature loves its own quality as the drunkard loves his cups, the gambler his cards, the thief his plunder. All may admit that sin is evil; but it has certain pleasures connected with it, and for the sake of these it is chosen. The corrupt affections want to be gratified, while they ought to be crucified.

5. The secular spirit hastens the decay of piety. It is like frost to a flower, rust to iron, the leprosy to man. If the world holds the soul, the soul holds the world. Fervor in religion, a strong faith, a bright hope, holy activity, are impossible if the secular spirit reigns. The ancients say that at Epirus there was a fountain which had the strange power of not only extinguishing a flame, but also of kindling one. Spirituality of mind will be sure to burn up worldliness,

while it will kindle into a flame those aspirations that seek for holiness and God.

6. A wayward imagination is another cause of decline in religion. The imagination is the gymnasium where souls are trained to vice. This faculty paints and pleases. When religious men startle others by a sudden plunge into evil, the work began in the imagination. Their deceptions, plots, and impure deeds flourished for a season in this unseen realm. It is a question even whether the fall of the first man was not hastened by the imagination.

7. Attachment to a particular sin will deaden the religious nature. A besetting sin may be the bane of life, producing the greatest misery. Sometimes there is an attempt to be exceedingly careful with a round of duties that are easy, so as to make up, as it were, for this sin that is difficult to manage. One may even dash off into a splended course of self-denial, thinking in this way to atone for the evil that will not die.

8. A want of childlike simplicity will start decay in religion. There is apt to hang around the soul a vast number of

fictitious appendages. The veritable man is hidden from view. He is buried beneath conventionalisms, forms of life, and a glare of appearances. Pure religion needs no art to decorate it. Holiness can not be made more beautiful than it is. Truth can not be improved. To be a man, one must be a child. The most gifted natures are distinguished for simplicity.

9. Religion declines when pure feelings are not acted out. When I feel that I ought to speak for God, be more benevolent, more circumspect in my dealings, and do not listen to the feeling, I harden the heart. If the great duties of the Christian life are pressed upon my attention, and I heed not the emotions that are awakened, I of necessity dampen and deaden the emotional nature. There is pleasure in mere feeling; and there is danger on that account that one will rest in it. If the church can be turned into a theatre, the pulpit into a stage, the minister into an acter, and the soul be thrilled by his words, all is well. Yea, if the feelings languish, and the accustomed ministration is not sufficient to move them, then a method that is startling and exciting

must be adopted. But what is all this but the Play of Death.

10. Sin viewed as enmity is the chief power that causes decay in religion. All the points that have been mentioned find their source in the malice that still lingers in the regenerate heart. "As every drop of poison is poison, and will infect, and every spark of fire is fire, and will burn; so the last and least particle of sin is enmity." It is because of this hating element that the good man feels partly disinclined to do his duty.

II. DECAY IN RELIGION FROM ERRORS OF THE MIND.

1. Decay in religion may be the result of misguided mental enthusiasm. A glow of pleasure may animate the understanding while engaged in close and consecutive thinking; but there is a want of balance. Truths of great moment are struck off, attracting the mind by the grandeur of their appearance, but alongside of them are errors fraught with evil. Still the errors are not seen. They have a certain clothing of majesty as if they were the children of light, and are listened

to as if they were the voices of God. There is no diminution of force as the heated intellect keeps at its work; yet there is a principle of decay eating into the moral nature. "When a large class of men," remarks Isaac Taylor, "is professionally devoted to the study of theology, there will not be wanting some whose mental conformation impels them to abandon the modest path of exposition, and to seek, within the precincts of religion, for the gratifications that accompany abstruse speculation, discovery, invention, exaggeration, and paradox. All these pleasures of a morbid or misdirected intellectual activity may be obtained in the regions of theology, not less than in those of mathematical and physical science, if once the restraints of a religious and heartfelt reverence for the authority of the word of God are discarded. The principal heresies that have disturbed the Church may, no doubt, fairly be attributed to motives springing from the pride or perverse dispositions of the human heart; but often a mere intellectual enthusiasm has been the real source of false doctrine." *

* "Natural Hist. of Enthusiasm," p. 82.

2. The influence of false philosophy tends to weaken the religious nature. There are few men who are able to view Christianity as it stands forth in its own divine singleness. They do not place the mind right in front of it, that that mind may be quickened by its full power. Commonly through some medium is the religion of Christ reached. We explain its doctrines by the aid of a particular system of metaphysics, and its commands by a particular system of ethics. No sooner had Christianity spread itself among the nations than the philosophies of heathenism rushed forward to corrupt it. The speculations about matter, mind, and God, were mixed up with Christian truth; so that speedily the religion of the New Testament was changed into another form, —half heathenism and half Christianity. It was next to impossible to find a person who had the pure religion of apostolic men.

3. When the soul loves the piety of abstract thinking, rather than the piety of moral action, there is a principle of decay at work. There are minds which desire to revel in a region of solitude where all is quiet, and where the urgent necessities of

life press not upon souls. It is not labor that pleases, but communion with thoughts of a certain order, losing one's self in the great abysses of being, breaking away as it were from matter and time. This mystical form of piety is seen in all ages. Especially is it seen during periods of strife and formalism. At such times the pensive spirit, weary of life, sinks into itself; hoping there to meet the good that it wants. Such a religion is one-sided. It is pale by reason of its seclusion and want of action. It reminds us more of the Hindoo contemplatist, than of the Christian soldier.

4. Reverence for things that are secondary, with no sufficient reverence for things of superior moment, generates decay. The history of the Church of the first centuries shows how religion was corrupted by undue attachment to secondary objects. The martyrs were honored above reason and above Scripture; and so there arose the adoration of relics, of idols, and of saints; the infinite God not receiving that worship that was due unto his name. A mystical and redemptive power was attached to the Christian sacraments; so that men approached

them as they approach the Most High. Thus their beautiful simplicity was lost. A class of artificial virtues soon appeared, and new sins troubled the consciences of men. An ascetic life was placed upon a level with the life of the angels, and the common tribe of disciples had to enter heaven by a less royal way. The laws and traditions of men were kept with greater strictness than the commands and teachings of God. A kind of human and materialized piety prevailed. The religious nature was in this way perverted; its strength was drawn off, and sent along subordinate channels.

5. A diplomatic form of piety weakens the Christian emotions. There is such a thing as tact and good judgment. These are to be used in well-doing. A blind goodness is wickedness. The want of discretion is sin. Still the religion of diplomacy is not the religion of Christ. There is something of the earthly about it. The jesuitical form of piety and the diplomatic, are of the same parentage. An attempt is made to extend the kingdom of Christ as men extend other kingdoms: namely, by

expediency and compromise. Sin is not viewed as so dark and holiness not as so bright, as they are in themselves. Good and evil are brought closer together by this means, and are made to treat each other with a degree of respect. The religious mind is thus contaminated. It is Christian and anti-Christian at the same time. Evils that were at first *condemned*, are afterwards *winked at*, then finally *approved*. There was not sufficient moral power to overcome the evils; and so, turning necessity into a virtue, they were pronounced to be good. In this way the world gains upon the Church, and in this way the diplomatic disciple sinks into the world.

When religion is popular and fashionable it declines. We are apt to think that when the bark of God is pressing ahead with flying colors, full sails, and every state-room occupied with gleeful people, that then all is prosperous. Great mistake. The Church and the world are two distinct companies. Christianity is popular in heaven. But upon this earth, where the whole race are lost, the religion of the Sinless One can not be popular. A religion that is fashionable is not a well-fashioned religion. If Satan is pleased with me, God is displeased.

6. When unconverted men are allowed to connect themselves with the Church, piety languishes. It certainly is a fact that Christianity during the early centuries went into an eclipse, and continued in that eclipse for more than a thousand years, because crowds of the unconverted became members of the Church. Such men are viewed as pious when they have no piety. Their influence, therefore, deceives and destroys. The good follow them as if they were good. Their practices are adopted; their opinions are praised; their pleasures find favor with unsuspecting souls. In a season not long the scale of piety sinks. Worldliness gains friends, and the friends of God become worldly. A pleasant formalism takes the place of religion. Men join the Church with faith in a creed, but with no faith in Christ. If they possess a few of the virtues of nature, these are accepted for the graces of the Spirit. The result of all this is, that men outside of the Church despise it, and men inside pull it down. The great enemy of the Church is the Church. Professed fol-

lowers of Christ are writing against Christianity. The Bible to them is too large, the supernatural too common, the atonement too painful, the sinful state of man too sinful, the way to heaven too difficult, the punishment of the wicked too long. That religion is blighted by such a state of things can not be denied. Although unconverted men will find their way into the Church, even when those who guard its portals are the most careful, no premium should be offered to tempt them thus to come. A smaller and purer Church will exert a far better influence on society, than one that is larger and more corrupt. Nothing succeeds, in the long run, like holiness. The Christianity of *appearance* covers a great surface and counts a great number; while the Christianity of *reality* is limited, yet strong with the strength of God.

III. Decay in Religion from a Deceived Conscience.

"Many species of the genus *Mantis*," says the Duke of Argyle, "are wholly modelled in the form of vegetable growths. The legs are made to imitate leaf-stalks, the body is elongated and notched so as to simulate a twig; the segment of the shoulders is spread out and flattened in the likeness of a seed-vessel; and the large wings are exact imitations of a full blown leaf, with all its veins and skeleton complete, and all its color and apparent texture. There is something startling and almost horrible in the completeness of the deception—very horrible it must be to its hapless victims. It is the habit of these creatures to sit upon the leaves which they so closely resemble, apparently motionless, but really advancing on their prey with a slow and insensible approach. Their structure disarms suspicion,"* These insects make us to think of a deceived conscience.

1. If I am under obligation to perform certain duties, while as yet I do not know what these duties are, the want of knowledge will cause my conscience to give forth a wrong decision. Thousands of pious men are not troubled in the least in regard to certain sins which they commit, because to them they are not viewed as sins. Ignorance, however, can not excuse me if knowledge is within my reach. Conscience is nec-

* "Reign of Law," p. 184.

essarily connected with the intellect; and to the extent that the judgment is sound the conscience is sound. There is a vast difference between Christian minds of a former age and those of the present in regard to temperance, the toleration of religious opinions, personal liberty, and the duty of carrying the gospel to the heathen. Certain things are now seen to be evil that were not seen before, and certain things are now seen to be good that were not seen before.

2. Natural traits which resemble those that are spiritual may deceive the conscience. The excitable Christian may think that he has more holy vitality than rightly belongs to him. He may give himself credit for unction in his prayers and in his speaking, and others may attribute the same quality to him, when the chief power at work is nervousness, along with a certain sweet tone of voice and a theatric manner. There are genial characters, persons who wear a sunny smile and manifest a fine cheerfulness, who may not allow sufficiently for these traits when they note down the amount of pure and heavenly joy. There are men who are distinguished by nature for gentleness and

amiability, who may seem to themselves holier than they are. Then we have the erratic and eccentric species, who take great liberties in speech and action. They have a kind of dashing and haphazard method; and evil is done when they know it not.

3. Prejudice is sure to deceive the moral faculty. If there be prejudice against certain truths, these truths will not be seen as they are. If one is prejudiced against certain methods of action, certain institutions of religion, certain duties to be done, he will be sure to form a false judgment. There may be prejudice also against certain persons; and this will so influence the mind that, however nobly they may act, there will be dissatisfaction with them. Thus a hating and hateful disposition will be cultivated. It was prejudice which led men to distort the life of Christ. Prejudice condemned him, and prejudice nailed him to the tree.

4. Near relationship may lead us to approve sinful acts in our friends. If the father of a family is acquiring wealth by certain questionable speculations, the children will be very apt to justify him in the

course he is pursuing. If we have a relative who owns a distillery, employs a large number of men, and treats them with great kindness, we shall be tempted to uphold him in his business. If any member of our household is making money by unnecessary labor on the Sabbath, we will be inclined to look charitably on this breach of God's law.

5. An evil that we condemned when it first appeared, may be approved when it is fixed into a habit. Familiarity with evil makes it to appear less hateful. While the bad habit was allowed to form, a golden haze spread over it, and conscience was led astray. The fact that we have permitted the evil to take possession of the soul and to hold there a kind of sovereignty, shows that we have been somewhat favorable to it. To the rule of the new power, therefore, we try to submit as gracefully as we can. Things are not as bad as we anticipated. To make defeat a virtue is now the effort of the soul. One does not love to condemn himself in that which he allows. We therefore take the final step and approve the bad habit. Certain evil customs in a community may come to be approved

in the same way, although at first they were condemned. If we are thrust into painful circumstances, and find it hard to escape from them, the mind shapes itself to these circumstances, and tries to feel comfortable.

6. The very tenacity with which one clings to an opinion or form of life may make it appear right, when in reality it is wrong. The fixed intention of the mind not to reconsider the matter, the absence of all fear, and the general satisfaction with our belief and life, delude the conscience. It would be a great gain to certain persons if they would allow themselves to doubt. The very backwardness to re-examine the principles that govern us is suspicious. It would seem as if we had a distant thought that the ground we stand on is not quite solid, and so we assume a decided tone in order to keep the mind steady. If there be great self-sacrifice connected with some duty, and we do not want to perform it, the tendency will be to shut it out with the thought, that it does not come within the range of our obligation. The unpleasant, however, is very often the right, while the pleasant is the wrong.

7. Selfishness tends to deceive the conscience. It is next to impossible to find a man who condemns himself for not being sufficiently benevolent. Covetousness and deception are just as sure to go together as night and darkness. The miser is sure that he is right, though not a single deed of love warms his heart. Selfishness will cause a man to affirm that he has no qualifications for certain positions; hoping in that way to escape the labors and responsibilities which he does not love; wishing also to appear humble, that thus he may have the credit of goodness.

8. Presenting a good reason for a course of action, when a bad reason was the governing one, the conscience is likely to be deceived. It very often happens that a number of motives combine their power in order to lead the will to act. There is a tendency, therefore, to select the best appearing motive, and present that as the reason for action; when, as matter of truthfulness, a vicious motive had the supreme control. The Pharisees no doubt convinced themselves that they revered the ancient prophets, inasmuch as they repaired and beautified

their tombs; and yet they had not the least sympathy with the life of those godly men. If a particular sin turns out better than was expected, the guilty person will quiet his conscience by looking at this favorable turn of affairs. Sometimes, by the intervention of God, heavenly benefits are linked on to the evil actions of man; and so the transgressor being attracted by these, views them as the fair result of his deeds.

9. Persons may be deceived by following the first impulse. An impulse at the moment may seem to be right, but when carefully examined it is found to be wrong. If the impulse is very exciting, there may be danger. Excitement may confuse the mind; things may not be looked at in their entireness; arguments may not be properly weighed; and so the person is led astray. The proper way, then, is to wait till the excitement passes over, that with composure and carefulness we may look the matter through and through. Having done this, we can decide upon the course that is best.

10. A first impulse, however, may be right, while the cool judgment may be nothing but sin. Robert Hall says: "In mat-

ters of prudence, last thoughts are best; in morality, your first thoughts are best." To let slip a true impulse of conscience, under the plea that we had better wait, is to become both weak and wicked. An excitation of love may come forth in a moment—pointing to an act that should be done, or a word that should be spoken—to follow that is both wise and good. The first impulse relating to some great moral questions is quite likely to be right, because selfish considerations have had no time to work. Even when the impulse is all on fire, we may yet follow its guidance with the utmost safety. There is no other way sometimes to perform a great religious act except under the influence of high excitement. The excitement breaks up the monotony of the soul, sweeps away the difficulties that lie across our path, urges us forward; and so we go and do that which is right. When the question was settled on Mount Carmel that Jehovah is God, and all the people were intensely excited, Elijah just at that time, himself under excitement, took the four hundred and fifty false prophets and put them to death. There is no likelihood that such a notable act could have been performed at any other time than that time of excitement.

11. Conscience may be deceived by good running into evil. The step from one to the other may not have been noticed. The spurious act or feeling may be so much like the true that suspicion is not awakened. (*a.*) The man who is decided may become over-bearing. The tendency will be to harshness and severity. It may not be long before decision ends in stubbornness. (*b.*) He who is earnest may become impatient. If other persons are sluggish, this annoys the earnest man. He begins to complain and condemn. The earnestness loses itself in ill-temper. (*c.*) Firm confidence may wander off into spiritual pride. Confidence and certainty go together; and so when a man sees that all is sure, he may become emboldened, highly elated, until his head swims with vain glory. The angels of heaven dropped from faith to pride. (*d.*) Gentleness may become weakness. A mild and unobtrusive character may lack force; and the lack of force leaves the soul in a state of passivity. The spirit that is gentle may at length be nothing but organized ease and softness.

(*e.*) Contentment need not go far before it reaches indifference. He who is troubled about nothing may very soon care about nothing. Care must be taken lest contentment be simply sanctified dullness. (*f.*) A long-suffering disposition may eat out boldness. There is a time for justice as well as for mercy. Long suffering may be long sinning. He who will not take sides with right, because of tenderness, has already taken sides with wrong. (*g.*) Caution may become timidity. Caution wants to risk nothing; but he who risks not gains not. I must not be rash; but if I halt, when I ought to hasten, I sin. (*h.*) Boldness may plunge headlong into rashness. The impetuosity of courage may so hurry the mind along that neither dangers nor difficulties are sufficiently considered. The bold words may lack judgment, and the measures adopted may lack wisdom.

CHAPTER VIII.

MEANS TO ARREST DECAY IN THE RELIGION OF CHRIST.

THERE is an *indirect* as well as a *direct* method of arresting decay in religion. In order to thoroughness of restoration, both methods must be adopted.

I. A VIEW OF THE PIETY OF THE EARLY CHRISTIANS A MEANS TO ARREST DECAY IN RELIGION.

"The device upon Whitefield's seal was a winged heart soaring above the globe; and its motto was, '*Astra petamus*'—Let us seek heaven." The early Christians were men of the winged heart. The very sight of them inspires us. An arrest is laid upon our sin by their presence. We approach the likeness of the object we are contemplating.

Their religion was *love*. The love seemed like a new production; as if it had come from a new world. It was not that of race or sect; not that of a mere sentiment, appearing in beauty for a day, and then at the close of it disappearing forever. It was a veritable power, burning with an energy like that of the sun, sending forth light and heat at the same instant of time. The love nad all the qualities of a divine affection. It was wise and discriminating, self-sacrificing and constant, free and pure. To the lost it was a friend, and to the friend it was a brother. The Creator by it was adored, the Saviour by it was trusted. Its strength did not depart in tears. If it lamented, it also labored. No more beautiful sight has ever appeared than the early community of Christ, cemented and hallowed by love. The affection took its rounded form as it were at once. It was clear as a mountain stream, and glad as the breeze of summer. Distance and coldness, calculation and shrewdness, do not appear in it. It is a single glory as that of a star. It is one of the rays of God. There is a certain sweet vehemence about the love; a kind of celestial freshness; nothing stereotyped; the whole natural and easy. We think of spring on a beautiful day. Trees of righteousness are covered with buds and blossoms. There is no wild manifestation. The life is not eccentric. It does not shoot forth and then rest; does not ebb and flow. The love is so normal looking that one is drawn towards it. The actions come in their time even as the moments and hours come. There is a certain originality about the experience which arrests the attention. The tide of love never rose so high before. It forms an epoch in history.

In the piety of the first Christians we notice an element of *simplicity*. There is a childlike spirit. Mere extrinsic glitter does not dazzle the eye. There is nothing tawdry and gairish. There is no attempt to produce a sensation. Many things that are common to other men are not seen in the early disciples of Jesus. The great central passion has burned up that which was superfluous, and left the character in a state of simplicity. We behold a species of holy condensation. A refining process has been at work. The alloy has been expelled. We gaze upon the simple pure article by itself, and are not startled by a multiform and showy greatness. A divine reduction has given to us the reality, and we are satisfied with it.

There is consequently a simplicity of heart, of manner, and of action. Not a single phase of the jesuitical spirit is seen in those first followers of Christ. They stand forth as Israelites indeed in whom there is no guile. They can not change virtues for sins and sins for virtues, in order to meet circumstances. The plotting and the underhanded do not characterize them. They were fine Christians; but had not the qualities to make fine politicians. Indeed, considering that so many of those people were converted *Jews*, we wonder why they had so much simplicity and so little cunning. Their divine lineage was more distinctly marked than their human. There was a plainness about them that looked like truth, and a sincerity that looked like righteousness.

The first disciples had a *firm persuasion* of the *truth* of Christianity. They were not governed by mere speculation; not led forward by the mere force of an opinion; but they stand in the presence of unmistakable facts, or in the presence of eternal ideas that had entered into time. They consequently act out of a consciousness that is sure and well defined. They arrest attention by this very fact of certainty. They break into fragments every false system and every false character by the simple blow of truth. The great chiefs of Christianity were men of undoubted faith, and so they communicated their spirit to others. The reign of belief in this way spread. Christians seemed to speak with authority; their voice seemed like the voice of God. All classes were told that "there is none other name under heaven given among men, whereby they could be saved," but the name of Jesus. This settled conviction in regard to the truth of Christianity was power itself. It not only conquered opposition, but it made the followers of Christ to feel that their religious experience was a reality. Thus objectively and subjectively Christianity was to them certain.

They exemplified the fact of *unity* with singular perfection. One thought possessed them; one feeling moved them; one purpose governed them. There was no mere outward uniformity thrust upon their attention, which they were compelled to adopt. The union came out of their soul, and expressed the spiritual state of the soul. They had such strength and purity of love that any thing else but oneness seemed to be a moral impossibility. It was not the pride of an order that held them together; not the sense of consistency; not the sense of duty. They were a real brotherhood of men; the only true brotherhood that had ever appeared. Persons talk about the cosmopolitan spirit; talk about unity, fraternity, liberty; not knowing that the first Church of Jerusalem illustrated these characteristics eighteen hundred years ago. Those noble people had simply one aim in life. They were gifted with the single eye. Power, therefore, was concentrated, and brought to a point. Nothing was wasted; there was no friction. They were a compact body filled with the Spirit; living for God; blessing men. Their Christianity was not a mere passive and contemplative form of life. Its field of effort was not the desert, the cave, or the solitary human spirit. When the first Christians were persecuted, "they went everywhere preaching the gospel." Religion with them was whole-souled. Its law was action, its nature benevolence, its sphere the world.

They showed also great *steadfastness* of

character and principle. There is a kind of theoretic steadfastness which one may have when all is pleasant. Soldiers during a time of peace arrange a mock battle. They fight bravely. But among all the victors not one is wounded, and among all the vanquished not one is slain. The Christianity of early times had to be realistic. It needed the utmost force and vitality. Evil was aroused, was alarmed, its empire was in danger. An attempt was made to overcome the new religion. To overcome it was impossible. There was an obduracy of principle that could not be conquered. He who is lost in God is never defeated. Both heathen and Jew were alike astonished, were alike maddened. The new superstition could not be reasoned with; the new moral malady could not be cured: there was no other way but death for the dangerous men. And yet even death itself failed; Christianity would not die. Tertullian, addressing the persecutors, says: "All your refinements of cruelty can accomplish nothing; on the contrary, they serve as a lure to this sect. Our number increases, the more you destroy us. The blood of the

Christians is the seed of a new harvest. Your philosophers, who exhort to the endurance of pain and death, make fewer disciples by their words, than the Christians by their deeds. That obstinacy, for which you reproach us, is a preceptor. For who that beholds it, is not impelled to inquire into the cause? And who, when he has inquired, does not embrace it; and when he has embraced it, does not himself wish to suffer for it?"*

A striking peculiarity of the early Christians was their *Christly* mind. Of course every disciple of Jesus has this characteristic to a greater or less extent. But the primitive Christians had it in a marked manner. Many of them had lived during the lifetime of the Saviour. They had seen him, heard him speak, and were cognizant of the wonderful works which he performed. He had impressed them as no one ever could impress them. He was to them "God manifest in the flesh." His image was reproduced in their souls. All that was dear to them in time and eternity was centered in him. He alone was their Saviour.

* Neander, "Church Hist.," vol i., p. 77.

His mysterious sorrow, agony, death, were remembered by them with tender affection. The fact that he rose from the dead, that he ascended into the heavens, could not be forgotten. He was the joy of their heart; the wonderful stranger who tarried with them for a season; the only kingly soul that they had ever seen, and whose glory lingered around them after he went away. Even those who had not beheld him, yet conversed with men who had. They were carefully taught in regard to his person and life. No doubt many a long evening was spent in listening to words he had spoken, and in hearing about the works he had done. Crowds met together on Sabbath and week day to catch the story of his life. No such Presence ever touched the souls of men before. Christ seemed to be in every dwelling of the faithful. His praises fell on the ear of friend and foe. There was no language but that spoke his name. He was a new thought in the great world of man. The night gave place to the day, and the gloomy empire of death was lost in the endless life.

The first Christians were *cheerful* in the

service of Christ. Their sky was clear. It was the early morning of their joy. In gladness the hours passed. In hope the noonday of heaven drew near. The sadness of other ages of the Church was not known among the first disciples of our Lord. They had a pleasure in piety which we have only seen occasionally; a peace which we know only at second-hand. At the very beginning "they received the word with gladness"; and so they went forward in the midst of happy emotions. It would seem as if a new cycle of supernatural power began at that time, and as if their souls received a great quickening from the Spirit of the Lord. "The disciples," we are told, "were filled with joy, and with the Holy Ghost." The whole range of Christian action gave evidence of life that had come from God, and of a certain sweetness and peace that were the result of it. The most common duties were hallowed by a new power: nothing was so small but that joy could smile around it. Those favored people could "eat their meat with gladness": they could serve or sleep with a heavenly serenity about their souls.

They were really a singular race of men; peculiar because of their saintliness. Their history all the way through would constitute an exceedingly interesting Pilgrim's Progress. "One might see them walking like so many pieces of immortality, dropping down from heaven, and tending thitherward; all full of God, and full of Christ, and full of heaven, and full of glory: and this world was nothing to them; trampled upon as a despicable, contemptible thing."* Their journey to the celestial city would not have the rural features about it which Bunyan's allegory presents. More of the city and town life would appear. A greater variety of characters would be seen along the way. The stir would be more intense, the temptations more numerous, the solitude not so deep. There would be seas also for the pilgrims to cross, and strange countries for them to enter. The commotion created by their appearance and manner would even be greater than in Bunyan's time. There would not be a solitary martyr as at Vanity Fair; but in Jerusalem and Rome many would die as witnesses for Christ. Some of the cities through

John Howe's "Works," vol. i., p. 580.

which the early pilgrims passed were noted for wisdom and wickedness. The town of Works was a busy place. Ladders were made there what would reach to heaven. There was a divine city called Jehovah Shammah, where the pilgrims dwelt for many days. It was near the end of the journey. They spent their time there with peacefulness. The country of God was just before them. They crossed the river of Death with joy. The sun shone upon them all the way.

Without attempting to specify all the spiritual traits of the first Christians, we may rest where we are, and simply add a few observations that are critical in their nature.

I suppose we have a right to say that the primitive Christianity was of a high type. In certain particulars, we may affirm that it has never been equalled. The golden age was at the beginning. In all succeeding centuries, men will look back upon a form of life that they have never seen elsewhere. They will sigh as they think of the early time, and will wonder why the former beauty shines not in any soul just now. It is a pleasure to them to regale their imagination with a sight that is so fair; the heavenly image they would like to make their own as the years run by. The model life which they would hold up before all the generations, is that of the first Christians. To bring the Church back to the primitive piety would be very much like restoring the lost Paradise. There is one extreme of making the early Christians better than they were, and another extreme of making them worse than they were. The point is to find the exact truth.

In looking through the New Testament, we notice that the *actual* and the *ideal* religion is each described, and that very frequently the one runs into the other. Sometimes in a chapter, referring mainly to the common life of the Christians, will be found a verse that pictures out the ideal religion with great beauty; and the danger is, that those very Christians will be viewed as possessing that ideal religion,—thus making them to be more holy than they actually were. Especially are we in danger when thinking of the inspired men who wrote the New Testament. We may very easily view them as quite angelic in their piety, just because of the ideal religion which they mention here and there. We are always tempted to clothe a writer or speaker with those holy qualities which he simply describes ideally. Thoughts are found in many sermons and many hymns that are instinct with seraphic beauty and perfection; and an uncritical person may be led to say that the writers of them were saintly men of a high order. Vast numbers, no doubt, have thus received a character, which never would bear the test of an actual examination. It is not that the writers intended to deceive. The thought was not in their mind to do that. They simply presented a finished conception; and unskilled persons supposed that that finished conception was a real gem that sparkled in their character. In descriptive writing especially, which relates to an object we love, the imagination with its fine ideals is very apt to do a great work at painting. We must see to it, then, that we find the actual truth in regard to the early Christians; not allowing any ideal glory to cover them with its celestial radiance. Even the common usage of language we must scrutinize carefully, lest a mere popular statement should be viewed as containing more than it really does contain.

It may have been a gain, and yet it may not, that the early Christians had no *past* in the religion they had adopted, to which they could look. It may be a blessed thing to be at the fountain-head, and to drink out of the rill that flows forth from the mountain's base; still there are many advantages in living upon the bank of a wide and deep river, far from its source; many advantages in commerce and wealth from the ships that trade at its ports. It is certainly a fact that we learn a great deal from the past. Its rich heritage comes down to us, and our present is enlarged because of it. It is an infinite gain to us that we can look back upon the achievements of Christianity during a period of eighteen centuries. Providence in the interest of the Christian religion is quite luminous, the administration of the Spirit is full of life and power, and the revelation of God to man is complete in the Bible. It would seem as if we had the means for a more extended type of piety than the early Christians had. There was about them a certain want of experience in many important things. There was a degree of immaturity that arose from their childhood state. They were in danger of being captivated by fair appearances. They were not sufficiently searching. Their faith might lead to credulity. There was weakness in connection with their strength. Germs of evil were ready to spring up by the side of their goodness.

Although they were a spiritually minded people, yet it is a question whether they were absolutely settled upon an extended basis of theologic truth. Was not the mould in which they were cast too limited, even though it was well finished as far as it went? Would not a greater range of thought have been to their advantage? Did they have a sufficient amount of individualism? Did all their faculties act with sufficient force, and was there a proper balance among them? We are to take into the account also that they lived during a great revival period. Hundreds and thousands were converted at once. It was the flood-tide of God's mercy to man. Possibly the waters of life never rose so high as at that time. The barks of Christ hastened forward with full sail and a fair wind. There was much that was *visible*. The good people could see and hear. The sense element was a notable feature. There were the gift of tongues and the various miracles. There was not merely a walking by faith, but a walking by sight. Taking these things into consideration, we are led to form a proper judgment touching the piety of the early Christians; making it not too bright, but still viewing it as of a very high order. We may well be stimulated by it, seeing by the contrast our earthliness and want of holy power. Yea, the Christian in a state of decline may even feel alarmed, when he beholds the force and the fervor of those first children of the Church.

II. Direct Method of Arresting Decay in Religion.

Thou great Being! make us like thyself. Thou only art real. All about us is illusion. We find no rest. We wander from object to object, but nothing pleases. Our very dreams tell of the wailing of our soul. We sink into the bosom of sleep with a sigh, and awake in the morning with the same burden pressing us down. Never are we quite well. Our sunniest hours have back of them a cloud. A thorn seems to be in the centre of our heart, and death struggles along the pathway of our life. Thou High and Lofty One! how much we need thee. Intervene in our behalf. Let thy smile banish our darkness, and thy breathing scatter our sin. Only when we are one with thee shall we be happy. Thou art the fountain of goodness. Blessedness dwells with thee. How wondrous thy years! No shadow of evil about thee! Only light and love! May some power touch us that will make us true and pure. We turn to thee. In exile we have wandered far and long. Only with thee can we feel well. Thou will not spurn us away. Why should we hold back? We take thee as our portion. In the midst of thy day shall we abide. Thy radiance shall gild our path, and the hours shall be full of joy because thou art near. Glorious One! the whole universe looks to thee. When thou hidest thyself there is trouble. Nothing can rest save as it rests in thee. If we seek for truth, thou art the True; for goodness, thou art the Good; for perfection, thou art the Perfect. Most ineffable Being! we can not describe thee. Only a few of thy words have reached us; a few of thy **rays have streamed across our path; thy** footsteps are echoing through the great silence, and thy beauty is painted on the flowers and skies of life. Thou art the ocean that has no storms, the land that is always fair, the river that flows in peacefulness through the smiling fields of love.

It is well to think of the *bright past.* This vision of other days may give the soul a new impulse. One can see how he has fallen. The sin appears the darker when contrasted with the holiness. As scene after scene is called up, when the soul was happy in God's service, there is a desire to begin a new life. Simply to mention over to a friend the season of our conversion; the number of persons who gave themselves to Christ at that time; the activity of Christian people; the solemn and searching preaching; the meetings so quiet and so crowded,—just to note these things warms the heart. "There is no more effectual means," says John Owen, "to stir up backsliders unto endeavors for deliverance than a continual remembrance of former things, and experiences they have had of holy intercourse and communion with God. This will revive, quicken, and strengthen the things that are ready to die, and beget a self-abhorrency in them in consideration of that woeful frame and temper of mind which, by their sins and negligence, they have brought themselves into." "I have known one in the depths of distress and darkness of mind, who, going through temptation to destroy himself, was relieved and delivered in the instant of ruin by a sudden remembrance that at such a time, and in such a place, he had prayed fervently with the engagement of all his affections unto God."*

A *vivid conception* of truth is also an important means of leading the soul into a higher life. The intellect and heart are closely connected together. If I would bring myself into a proper moral state, as far as I am able, there are three things that are necessary. 1. I must have a suitable object before the mind. 2. I must have a vivid conception of that object. 3. I must act out the feeling that is generated by this vivid conception. The central and moving power is to *feel*. I must set the imagination to work, and make the whole matter as real as possible; then emotion will be started.

* "Works," vol. vii., pp. 465, 466.

Let a mother behold her children in a house on fire; and she will be carried away with a tempest of feeling, and will do her utmost to save them. If she were sound asleep, she would neither feel nor act. Let any one witness the collision of two trains of cars; see the wounded, dying, and dead; hear the cries of suffering people as they beg for help,—there will be no want of feeling. "Agitate the soul in any way, excite its fears, hopes, or any of the passions, and then instantly, and *just in proportion to the excitement*, will the mind lose its consciousness of all but the single exciting object. Show a man the muzzle of a loaded cannon, peeping from a thicket in the distance, and whence he may every moment expect his death; show him, on the broad bosom of a tumbling sea, an open boat, in which his wife and children are tossing, between hope and despair, and what else will he see!"

Christian men are palsied with indifference because they do not face the truth in all its roundness. They do not compel themselves to think about it. No full impression is made upon their soul. They think in fragments, and feel in fragments. If for one hour they would look into the great realities of human life and the destinies beyond, they could not help but feel intensely. A single great utterance that strikes the soul like a voice from heaven, produces a wonderful effect. The more real I can make any truth, the more power it has. That which ennobles a man is the noble thoughts which he has. There is a mastering power in great ideas. They grasp the soul, hold it steady, send life through it. A great intellectual awakening is the usual precursor of a spiritual awakening. The flame of primitive Christianity was kindled by the imperial thoughts of God and Christ. The herald of the Reformation was truth. Methodism was ushered into existence by the power of divine ideas. The great missionary movement commenced when light touched the souls of the good. Even upon the low plane of humanitarianism, men are aroused by a vivid conception of the truth which belongs to that sphere. When the people are stimulated in regard to national integrity, it is evident that they have been thinking about that matter. Perhaps in no organization of man has close and continued thought done so much as in the organization of the Jesuits. Their "spiritual exercises," hour after hour, day after day, for weeks, turn out a race of sharp, devoted, and most determined men. If intense thinking has done so much to mould and marshal into line the followers of Loyola, how much more should intense thinking mould and marshal into line the followers of Christ. Let truth be comprehensive, let it be well balanced, let it flash upon the soul with its own eternal light, then it will surely affect the heart, mind, and conscience, in a healthy manner. If the law of God in its length and breadth were more correctly studied by the disciples of Jesus, they would be a finer and more finished race of men than they have thus far been. The delusions of the moral faculty, the errors of the intellect, and many sins of the heart, are the result of imperfect views of divine truth.

In ancient times there was a race in the evening, at which the runners carried torches or lamps; and these were lighted at the sacrificial altar. Not only had the men to run, but they had to use great care and skill lest the light should be extinguished. If the lamps went out, the prize was lost. So the Christian must run, and he must exercise a sound judgment at the same time. He must be in haste, but not self-confident; must run, but not in pride. Generally speaking, however, the faster the Christian runs, the brighter his lamp burns. Only the indolent are left in darkness; only the indolent lose the prize.

If decay in religion is to be arrested, we must act very much as we did act when we *began the Christian life*. We must pass through the same stages of experience. The way the sinner takes before he can find peace and purity, is the way that we must take before we can find them. The initial point is to be aroused, startled out of our sleep. The sense of danger may sound the alarm. The possibility of losing the soul may strike it with terror. A new unhappiness may agitate our whole being. There is a sense of sin. Indeed, it would seem as if our feeling in regard to sin must be more deep and pungent than when we first repented. We have had a new experience of its evil; have seen how it has battled with goodness in the heart; have looked at it through the medium of a brighter light than we formerly had,—thus understanding it better, we have a deeper conviction. Possibly one reason why we have such feebleness in our Christianity, is because we have such feebleness in our views of sin. A profound consciousness of moral evil will lead us to prize highly the divine method of redemption. The Christian who takes a lame view of sin will be a cripple all his days. It is all-important that when we return to God we should have a deep feeling of guilt. This will lead us to abhor sin, and to turn from it. The penitent Christian also feels the need of redemption more than ever, and so he renewedly gives himself away to Christ. Thus the chief features of the early experience are reproduced. The child of God is awakened, he is convicted, he repents, he believes. In fact all these characteristics appear during every great crisis and onward movement of the Christian life. Even at the moment of death, when reason is clear, there will be a new awakening, a new conviction, a new repentance, and a new faith.

In order to keep my Christianity at the point which it has now reached, I must cultivate the power to *receive*. My entire soul must be thrown open to that which is pure. A receptive mind lies at the foundation of a holy character. Christ pronounced those blessed who were poor in spirit. Influences of goodness come up to my soul: I must give them free and happy admission. Many a saintly word falls upon my ear: I must listen to it. Here are biographical sketches of most excellent men: I must allow the influence of their life to reach my heart. Fine characters I see every day: I must be made better by them. There is Christ! What a world of goodness streams forth from him! I must surely become more holy on account of it. There is God! What a power he is! It would seem as if he must transform the soul. There is the Spirit! How I must receive that saving influence which he brings to me, or be lost forever.

I am to cultivate also the power to *form*. This power to form is very extended. The works of God in all their infinite variety are manifestations of his forming power. Even man, fallen though he be, is a great former. In architecture, painting, sculpture, useful inventions, literary productions, the bright ideals of the mind, we behold the forming power. Chiefly, however, in the sphere of piety, I am to form. If I can form a thought that will strengthen the soul in goodness, I have done that which is praiseworthy. If I can form a single grace like humility or patience, tenderness or temperance, I have done that which will tell upon the eternal well-being of the soul. Power to form a character is far greater than power to build the pyramids. And if I can form other souls besides my own, prepare them for an eternity at God's right hand, that is heavenly work. If I can form a hymn, a tract, a book, that will live for ages, blessing human spirits all that time, I have done that which angels might covet to do. Even if I can not go as far as this, but yet can form a prayer that will enter into the ear of God, can form a sentence that will honor the Saviour, can form a purpose that will steady the soul in the midst of the turmoil of evil—just that will be a power in goodness. Sin must be hindered in some way or another by the formative ability of the Christian mind. If I cease to form I cease to live.

By such means decay in piety is arrested. There is health and activity. The reformed Christian is ready for every good work. The life which he lives shows that he is changed. He feels humbled in view of the past. He carries about with him a deep sense of unworthiness. He is watchful and circumspect. He has had a sufficient experience of his own weakness; he therefore depends more completely on the Infinite Strength. If some leading sin carried him away while in a state of declension, the reaction is so great that it will never be committed again. He is an entirely new man since that terrible fall. One almost thinks that God permitted him to make a plunge, that he might rise the higher afterwards. Peter was a nobler man after his denial of Christ than he was before.

In whatever relation the revived disciple now stands, principle is set to work in that relation. He can not be bought, can not be sold, neither does he attempt to buy and sell other men. He is a man among men; quite above the common run; near to the great verities of life; on his way to the city of the angels; happy only in principle, and sad when he fails. He gives encouragement to no practice that is contrary to the gospel of Christ. He sees that what all men want, more than any thing else, is principle. Let this be found in business, in courts of law and conventions, in schools and legislatures, in every heart of child and man, then there will be prosperity. It is not money, but principle; not honor, but principle; not pleasure, but principle. When principle fills each office, each calling in life, is the inmate of every house and every heart, then joy will smile like the skies of heaven, and peace will reign over the untroubled years of time. Seest thou a man with principle?—he shall stand before the great with humility, and before the humble with greatness. His steps shall not falter in all his journey; strong shall he be with strength that never dies; and with hope beckoning him onward, he shall be happy in all the sweep of his years. His eye shall not be dim through all the length of his way, neither shall his mind be left in darkness; for the golden sun shall pour his radiance into it, and there shall be light and gladness through the ceaseless beat of the hours.

The working week shall be like the Sabbath, and the Sabbath like the rest of the angels. The labor shall flow on with love as if it were one of the hymns of God, and the very beating of the heart shall be a prayer that brings down blessings upon souls.

We can never be poor if we have principle; never ignorant if we have it: it forms the chief wealth and the chief wisdom. We never can be in solitude if we have it, for it is one of the best friends of God; neither can we be unhappy, for it is blessedness itself. Try as we may, we shall never be well without principle. Nothing can ever take its place. If we seem to succeed by something else, it is only a gilded deception. We may be cheated for a moment, but the end is death. Principle never fails. It is the only thing that makes heaven. God would not be God if he did not have it. Our real value is shown by our principle; and we are worth neither more nor less than that.

CHAPTER IX.

LAWS OF PROGRESS IN THE RELIGION OF CHRIST.

THE first law of progress points to the fact that religion is carried forward through the medium of *groups*. The religious germ is complex. If I say that piety consists in love to God, that does not imply that it is confined to one feeling. The love includes within itself a number of spiritual forces and tendencies. If I say that the essence of piety is pure obedience, that is equally comprehensive. If I call it a divine life in the soul, there is still more than unity. The truth is, the moment we have religion, that moment we have a group of powers at work. Different kinds of knowledge, different kinds of emotion, different kinds of action, find a place in that nature we call regenerate. As religion advances, therefore, it advances through the medium of groups. Each peculiar force works out in its own way, diffuses its vitality, gains victories, or, for the moment, simply holds its own. In fact every leading movement of the mind is complex. We talk about single thoughts and feelings; but the singleness is chiefly in name. We call the soul a unit; and in one sense it is a unit; but in another sense it is the source of possibilities that are well nigh infinite. Although man is a distinct individual, yet not in singleness does he work out his destiny. Progress in good or evil, in knowledge or ignorance, is by a system of grouping. Two or three errors will ruin a man just as effectually as a hundred. Let a person take a false view of himself, of God, and of Christ, and he is gone. Upon a vast number of other subjects he may be sound or unsound: this will make no essential difference as far as the chief facts are concerned. The few errors decide the case; decide it forever. A man may reach a crisis in his history. During this crisis he may examine carefully his form of belief. As the result of this examination he rejects a vast number of untruths. Still, if he retains a few that are leading in their character, there is no hope for him. Judas was lost by a few bad tendencies: the penitent thief was saved by a few that were good.

If I look now at religion viewed as a divine kingdom, I can see that it moves forward through the medium of *groups of men*. A few guiding spirits march first, and the multitude fall into line and follow after them with greater or less willingness. In each local church a small company of persons are the source of power. They plan, organize, toil, and pray. Let them die or depart into another region, and the church sinks. If it were a law that every religious person must act before the kingdom of God could move forward, it never would move forward. Thus far at least, groups of select souls have done the work. "The new life of a period of restoration," says Isaac Taylor, "takes its rise in the spirits and hearts of a few—a two, or three. Greater than any 'tendency of events' is the mind of this and of that man—born, and taught, and moved onward from above."* It is the two or three gathered together that can claim the blessing. In the theological sphere and the missionary sphere the chiefs have opened up the great lines of thought and action; and the millions, startled by their energy and

---

* "Logic in Theology," p. 285.

influence, move apace. In fact the development of the race in all its branches has been through the medium of groups of men. In arts and arms, literature and government, science and trade, a few choice minds are the powers. Even in the matter of public sin or wholesale wickedness, the magnates walk first. There are hosts of inferior spirits who are contented with a secondary place in schemes of daring iniquity. It is fair to suppose that as the Church advances, the groups of men who lead it forward shall be larger, purer, and more powerful. The time will no doubt come when the entire kingdom of Christ shall be a compact body of faithful souls.

The second law of progress shows that religion is developed according to a *threefold* principle. There is first the divine life, then the growth of that life, and still again the perfection of that life. We have thus a distinct beginning, progress from that beginning, and completion as the result of that progress. There can be no such thing as the evolution of life without a germ. Life must come from life. I can not evolve something out of nothing. I can only draw forth that which exists: never more than that. Having found the germ, development is possible, development is a fact. As we look at the vegetable kingdom, the march of life is seen to be according to the number three. There is the seed, the growth from that, then the season of maturity. What is worthy of attention, the third stage is always *double*. As if one face were looking over the past which has gone, and another face were looking into the future which has not yet come. When the fruit is ripe, it does not remain on the tree forever. Being fully ripe, it falls to the ground. There it takes root in the earth and forms a new beginning; the life always governing itself according to the triad movement, and the last member of the triad always containing a duality. It is somewhat significant that the work of the third day of the creation was double. There was the gathering together of the waters, and the appearance of vegetation: this double fact making known to us the end of the inorganic period, and the beginning of the organic. The work of the sixth day, this being the closing up of a second triad, is also double. The higher animals are created; and man makes his appearance upon the stage; man accountable, immortal, made in the image of God. Lepsius tells us that the Egyptian year had three seasons. The first was symbolized by a *reservoir*, the second by a *garden*, and the third by a *house*. The human race has its three cycles,—childhood, youth, and manhood. We notice also three leading dispensations,—the Patriarchal, Jewish, and Christian. In these we see the family, the nation, the world. The individual has a threefold system of training. "In childhood we are subject to positive rules which we can not understand, but are bound implicitly to obey. In youth we are subject to the influence of example, and soon break loose from all rules unless illustrated and enforced by the higher teaching which example imparts. In manhood we are comparatively free from external restraints, and if we are to learn, must be our own instructors. First come rules, then examples, then principles. First comes the law, then the Son of man, then the gift of the Spirit. The world was once a child under tutors and governors until the time appointed by the Father. Then, when the fit season had arrived, the Example to which all ages should turn was sent to teach men what they ought to be. Then the human race was left to itself to be guided by the teaching of the Spirit within." *

The third law of progress shows that religion advances by *epochs*. The thought here is different from that of the previous one. The development is not confined to the number three. The epochs are of no certain number. They may be few or many; the person and his surroundings, as well as the law which directs the bestowment of grace, making a difference. Religious characters in one age and nation may pass through various stages of spiritual life, while those in another age and nation may have a development that is peculiar to themselves. There are Christian souls whose life is remarkably even. It seems like a continuous chapter, with no breaks of any kind. Still, when carefully examined, there are varied sections. In other persons the stages of development are clearly marked. They pass through many seasons of revival during a

* "Essays and Reviews," p. 5.

lifetime. These are remembered as periods of strong faith, bright hope, warm-hearted love, free and pleasant activity, healthful joy and peace. There are some epochs of holy life which are caused by afflictions, by new and striking truths, a higher form of thoughtfulness, a sudden inflow of grace from the heart of God. There may be epochs also that signalize the appearance of the missionary spirit within us, a more divine conception of the Sabbath, a profounder sense of eternal things than we ever had before, a truer view of life and man than we ever have been accustomed to exercise. Change of place, entering upon some new relation, may each introduce a new section of development.

As we look at the kingdom of Christ, we can see that different epochs have marked its progress. The Pentecostal outpouring of the Spirit was a new stage; the great persecutions occasioned another; the Reformation under Luther was a notable epoch; the religious awakenings of the past century and the present have formed a striking chapter; the missionary and temperance movements show specific sections of life. The history of Christian doctrine is marked in the same way by epochs. We see how the doctrine of God comes forth, the person of Christ, human nature and divine grace, the atonement, justification by faith, the inspiration of Scripture. The present may even be called the Christological age. Sharp conflict rages around the character and person of our Lord. In the next century a system of pneumatology may be wrought out,—the Divine Spirit being the centre of interest. Possibly in the coming ages there may be a more complete development touching the millenium and the second coming of Christ than we have yet seen. It may be a question also whether a full and final statement of the atonement and original sin has yet been reached. The future may throw some light upon these doctrines.

Epochs of development are characteristic of nations. The various languages and laws show stages. There are periods of art and education, of simplicity and morality, of peace and freedom. There are epochs which tell of solid thinking, of strict rule and certain punishment, of poetry and fine taste, of great daring and enthusiasm. There are scientific and critical ages; ages of discovery and invention; practical and speculative ages.

Taking the human race as a unit, its progress is marked by stages. We may view the human race as *one man*. This worldman is about six or seven thousand years old. His life is very different to-day from what it was before the flood. When that judgment of God struck him, he nearly perished in his sins. He is very much larger and wiser at present than when he came forth from the ark. He has also more of good and evil about him than he had then. Even in the space of two or three thousand years, he has advanced exceedingly. Yea, within the period of a few hundred years, he has astonished himself by the rapidity of his development. When we look in this way at the one universal man, having an organic life, as never having died, we see quite clearly the progress he has made; while at the same time we see his many falls, see that he has never been really well, notice his great restlessness, the mighty wars with himself, his attempts to gain health and happiness, but never quite succeeding. The earth itself on which he has lived seems almost to be the counterpart of himself; trying in its own strange way to mimic him in its movements. The ocean quiet to-day, and excited to-morrow, just as he is himself. Then the moaning of the winds in the darkness, making an effort to utter his complaint. The bursting forth of volcanoes, making us to think of his anger. The beautiful night in the spring-time when he seems to be asleep. The gardens covered with flowers as if they were children of the angels who had come to smile along his path. His strange dreams as he thinks of rest and of home; of the life that is never to end, and of that Infinite One who alone can give peace.

The fourth law of progress points to the fact that religious development is *antithetic.* Christian progress is not in a straight line. It is not sufficiently natural and normal to reach that ideal. The fact of sin in human nature, even after one is changed, hinders the development and makes it one-sided. The good man never presses forward but that he is held back to a certain extent. He may be fired with a glowing enthusiasm, and be most resolute in his determination, yet a degree of weakness and waywardness checks him in his course. There is a divine force in his soul, but wind and tide are against him; and so his progress is antithetic. Like many a ship crossing the ocean, he meets opposing currents and fierce gales which drive him from the straight course. As the sailing vessel has to tack many a time, going this way and that in order to gain a little, so is it with the Christian in his passage to heaven. The log-book of a ship describes the soul's voyage to the Land of Glory. It is unusual to have a smooth sea and fine weather during the whole passage. Days pleasant and unpleasant, nights dark and clear, the speed fast and slow, characterize the voyage. Sometimes one even loses his reckoning, and can not tell where he is. By and by the sun comes out, and with that his true position, and so he is filled with joy. Hope and fear, grief and gladness, faith and unbelief, pain and pleasure, mark the history of the religious mind. Our progress is conditioned by a law of antagonism. In the midst of contraries we are to fight our way. He who gains the victory shall be saved. The ideal progress will be seen in the eternal kingdom of life.

There is no development upon earth except that which is antithetic. The vapor ascends and the rain falls. The very light comes to us in waves. Sound trembles in its journey through the air. Our blood beats in its passage. We are conscious and unconscious, remember and forget, sleep and awake, live and die. The earth has its day and night, its summer and winter. Knowledge and civilization are never uniform. Man individually and collectively goes by starts. Activity and indolence mark his way. There are bright and dark ages, progress and retrogression, revolution and repose. Empires rise and fall, races live and disappear. If a distinguished father seldom has a son as distinguished as himself, so a noted period of history is seldom followed by one that equals it. The first age of Christianity was purer than the second. The seventeenth century in England showed greater mental and spiritual power than the eighteenth. It is doubtful whether the twentieth century will equal the nineteenth in fruitfulness of thought and invention. Thus a people strong to-day are weak to-morrow, and a people weak to-day are strong to-morrow. The pride that echoes our greatness is the beginning of our relapse, and the humility that proclaims our nothingness is the first step of our ascending march. Glory in truth for truth's sake, may have wrapped up in it self-sufficiency and hatred of God. The waving banner of our bravery may simply tell of our defeat. Our life may be death. There is a wisdom which is not wise, a goodness not good, a happiness not happy. The weak are the strong: the lost are the saved.

Christian progress is something like a winding staircase that leads to the top of a high monument. It is like a road that is cut around a great mountain; ascending little by little, till finally after severe labor the summit is reached. Religious development takes the spiral form. The position of leaves on the branch of a tree illustrates the principle. "The spiral line of development as the initial in evolution," says Dr. Dana, "and retained in its perfection in the spiral arrangement of leaves in plants, as well as in the parts of some animals, is a grand law which science has evolved from the mass of facts in the plant kingdom. And this law has its more special announcements: follow the leaves, from one leaf (A) as a starting point around the stem, taking the course of the spiral to another leaf (B) in the same vertical line with the first; and if there are two or three leaves in the spiral, the spiral goes around but once before reaching leaf B; if there are five leaves in the spiral, the spiral revolves two times before it reaches leaf B; if there are eight leaves, it revolves three times; if thirteen leaves, it revolves five time; if twenty-one leaves, eight times; and so on, and the converse, by an inflexible rule. Placing the number of *leaves above*, and number of *turns below*, the following series expresses the relation:—$\frac{2}{1}$ $\frac{3}{1}$ $\frac{5}{2}$ $\frac{8}{3}$ $\frac{13}{5}$ $\frac{21}{3}$. Now the last eight, the number of revolutions for a spiral of twenty-one leaves, is the sum of five and three of the two next proceeding spirals in the series; and twenty-one, of thirteen and eight of the same two proceeding spirals. In this way the series extends on, in exact mathematical relation." * Although Christian development takes the spiral

* "Bibliotheca Sacra," vol. xiii., p. 85.

form, yet it has not that regularity and completeness that are seen in the arrangement of leaves in the plant kingdom. The movement upward is zigzag. There may even be a sinking down for a time by reason of some great sin: then there is a rising again by repentance and love to a higher plane of life than was reached before. There is a gain finally, though not a gain, perhaps, each hour or day. The Christian Church has made progress in the long run; yet certain years and ages show a manifest decline. Places that once had the gospel, now have it not; and places that once had not the gospel, now have it. There is a "geographical march" in religion, as well as in history generally. It is safe to affirm that there is more of vital Christianity to-day than ever existed before; a greater number of pious souls now upon the stage than ever flourished during any previous century.

The river that took its rise in Eden has never ceased to flow. The heat of summer has never dried it, and the cold of winter has never frozen it. Millions of people have quenched their thirst out of it in the ages of the past, and millions more will drink out of it in the ages to come. The river is wider and deeper than it was at the beginning. Indeed, it seems almost at certain places to be a great sea. The fountain that burst forth from Calvary has increased the volume of its waters; and that fountain never abates on any day, for a stream flows forth from it greater than ever before. The river is not straight, except at a few points. It winds around hills, goes through valleys, and over plains as the case may be. As one looks at it from the mountains of God, it is very beautiful. Trees of life grow along its margin; and the fruit of them is like to that which they have in heaven; and the leaves are always green. In future centuries the river will flow around the earth. It will then be called the Heavenly River; for the people who live upon its banks will be very pure, and the angels shall abide with them through all the years.

The fifth law of religious progress shows that development is from *fewness* to *manifoldness*. Beginning with the first principles of love, penitence, and faith, we are to go forth to an extended multiplicity. The initial stage of development is always simple;

always working in a narrow sphere. The different civilizations of the past had fewer characteristics about them, than have the civilizations of the present. Even the life of a hundred years ago had a simplicity and plainness which we see not in our day. The nations most assuredly have entered upon a new cycle of development. Manifoldness is the characteristic of the present. There may not always be depth, not always soundness, yet there is a most astonishing multiplicity. We have in many cases a grievous number of wants, a host of painful desires, a restless rushing after things that profit us not. The souls of the time seem to be more intense and hungry than the souls of the early ages; yet the food which they need they do not always find; and so they roll and dart away as the vexed fish in the wastes of the sea. Christianity must be manifold. It must touch human nature at every point. It must have a kind of omnipresence. Grace must be added to grace. "Progress," says Professor Guyot, "is *diversification*. Homo-geneousness, uniformity, is the elementary state. Diversity, variety of elements, which call for and multiply exchanges; the almost infinite *specialization* of the functions corresponding to the various talents bestowed on every man by Providence, and only called into action and brought to light by the thousand wants of a society as complicated as ours,— these have, in all times, been the sign of a social state arrived at a high degree of improvement." * There must be a spiritual wealth about the new man. He should have an interest in all that is good. No virtue must be wanting, no course of training forgotten, no self-denial passed aside. What a scene of development takes place from the time the seed is planted in the ground, until the time when the seed has become a tree and is loaded with fruit. What a picture of manifoldness is such a tree! How it symbolizes a good man; points to progress and perfection. If we could look upon the rude materials which were designed for some great cathedral, and then look upon the cathedral after it was finished, we should be astonished. The multiplicity and elaborateness on the one hand, and the fewness and roughness of substances on the other, would startle us by the con-

* "Earth and Man," p. 97.

trast. What a vast number of thoughts would such an edifice show forth! The Christian mind and character should be emblemized by such a noble fabric.

Not merely by righteous deeds are we to extend and beautify the character, but by using the wondrous *variety of divine truths* that meet us on the pages of the Bible. There is not a single Christian doctrine, however mysterious it may be, but that can be turned into a practical channel. New views of God and salvation, of law and duty, will generate a new class of feelings, and will enrich greatly the soul. If we reject any single doctrine of Christianity, which to our mind is not a doctrine of Christianity at all, then we suffer in our character. Each divine thought was designed to have a place in fashioning and fitting us for heaven. There may be phases of God's sovereignty and severity which we do not heartily admire; and so we may aim to soften them down as not in harmony with our ideal of a Perfect Being: but just to the extent that we do this, we sink in the scale of moral excellence. The most complete men are those who have allowed the totality of divine truth to touch their souls. The more we come in a line with the grand theology of Scripture the more we approach the perfection of God. If there be phases of the divine administration that baffle us, then let these very phases develop in us a feeling of awe and submission. A God that is squared to match with the finite and fallen reason of man, is sure to be no God at all. There are difficulties everywhere. To escape from them is not possible. The very difficulties may discipline the soul, making it stronger forever. It is wise, then, to grasp every form of truth, that the human spirit may be made complete. When we look at Christ, we can see the manifoldness of his character. He showed no mark of immaturity and contractedness. The one-sided and unfinished were not his. He dwelt in the midst of truth; was Truth itself. Each perfection shone in his life. Each virtue found a home in his heart. To approach his image is our labor. To reach that image is heaven.

CHAPTER X.

TO ADVANCE IN THE RELIGION OF CHRIST DEMANDS STRENUOUS EFFORT.

THERE is evidently a law of limitation in the bestowment of divine grace, making it necessary for every Christian to struggle to the utmost. Although remedial powers may be said to be co-extensive with the divine nature, yet, in using these powers, there is a principle of caution and economy. There are no trade-winds of love which sweep passive souls onward till heaven is reached. Salvation by grace is not salvation through the medium of indifference. If we use our moral power at any given time, God will give us more; but, if we are sluggish, darkness surrounds us. Even Christ was pressed to the utmost limit of human endurance Although all the resources of the Godhead were his, there was some great law that conditioned and measured their use. How can we explain the fact that he was in an agony, except upon the supposition that divine strength could only be used by him to a certain extent. If the Redeemer had wrought out salvation with ease, then with ease souls might have been saved. It would seem almost as if redemption were an exceptional thing in the system of God, and as if it must be guarded with great care lest evil should come out of it. When we look at the matter of doing good, we can see plainly enough that this is not by any means an easy thing. The march of Christianity in this world has been slow. Men have had to toil long and painfully in order to accomplish a little. We are to be possessed with a great thought, and with that great thought firing and fixing our souls we are to go forward. Yet when we have done our best, the suggestive words sound through our being—" The righteous *scarcely* are saved." They do enter heaven, but that is all. To some Christian souls there may be twelve degrees of grace, to others twenty, to others one hundred, and even to some royal spirits there may be one thousand; but each has somewhat according to his manner of life. God can do no more than he has done in the case of any religious man. Every thing shows, therefore, that we must be intent in the matter of our Christianity.

Two leading powers in the development of the race, have been the *sense of profit* and the *sense of pleasure*. Look at man in a rude state. If clothing is needed, the individual provides it for himself. If a hut is wanted, he constructs one. Tools, weapons of defence, cooking utensils, furniture, ornaments, are all made by himself. It is seen, however, after a time, that labor can be divided with great benefit to all concerned. Consequently there appear carpenters, masons, weavers, tailors, shoemakers, traders, and many others. A man feels that it is more profitable and pleasant to confine his attention to one thing. By concentration of effort, articles are perfected, cheapened, and thus rendered more accessible. Under the impulses of profit and pleasure, one man chooses one calling, and another man another calling. Each is anxious to gain as much wealth as he can, and as much comfort as he can. There are persons who change from one branch of in-

ADVANCEMENT DEMANDS EFFORT.

dustry to another, because they think that the change will be more agreeable and profitable to them. Men go from the country to the city, and from one state to another, under the influence of the same motives. Inventions are multiplied, commerce is extended, machinery is set in motion, at the bidding of profit and pleasure. Sometimes one of these motives will be made subordinate to the other. A man may see a fortune before him which can only be reached through the medium of suffering: he is willing to suffer. Another man tired with the rush after wealth sinks into indolence: the love of ease to him is a sweet joy.

Entering, then, the sphere of Christian discipline, we are met by these two principles of action. They seek to govern us; seek to neutralize our piety; seek to humanize it as much as possible. Religion, however, is not mere profit and pleasure. Holiness is the chief thing; the expulsion of sin the chief thing. To allow one's self to be governed by the agreeable and the profitable is easy; but to strike out upon a course of righteousness is difficult. At the beginning of the Christian life I can see that pain is the condition of purity. I am beset with cravings that I must deny; and to deny these cravings is not pleasant. Here are appetites of fearful power; appetites that have ruined millions; and I must keep them in their proper place. A system of materialism is outside of me, capable of generating both painful and pleasant sensations, and I must make it subordinate. In the human soul is the love of power, the love of honor, and the love of action—these must be regulated. Even the affections that centre in the family, the nation, and the race, have to be watched. Then there is ignorance and selfishness that we must fight against. Considering the vast power and range of depravity in the soul, the drill in holiness is not easy. Whether a man wants a vigorous intellect or a vigorous heart, he must suffer pain. Neither a scholar nor a saint can be formed without severe discipline.

We must say this, however, that so long as goodness is practised under a sense of pain, there is weakness and imperfection. "We must make the pleasure or pain," says Aristotle, "which follows after acts a test of the habits; for he who abstains from the bodily pleasures, and in this very thing takes pleasure, is temperate; but he who feels pain at it is intemperate; and he who meets dangers and rejoices at it, or at least feels no pain, is brave; but he who feels pain is a coward."* The pain is a sign that evil is trying to hold its own; and, so long as it exists, it shows that the evil is not conquered. The aim, then, must be to reach a stage of development when pain shall give way to pleasure. Not till moral action and joy come together is there a right state of soul. Many things in life are painful at first; but by continual practice they become pleasant. So long as I have to urge my soul to duty by the most stirring motives, that shows that I am weak: but when I can obey God from pure willingness, that shows that I am strong.

Still, while I am in the imperfect state, I must make myself do what I do not want to do. The will must go forth into action at the command of the purest motives, at the very time motives of an opposite character are striving to hold it back. A disagreeable duty may consist in beginning a

* "Nicom. Ethics," p. 37. Bohn's ed.

course of action which has been left unbegun for years; it may consist in restoring money that was taken by fraud; in forsaking companions that have never done me any good; in asking forgiveness of a man whom I have injured, or in treating a man kindly who has injured me. "The young Scythian was bound to drink the blood of the first enemy whose life he had taken; and he who had not drunk of this horrible draught was condemned to sit apart in the great festivals presided over by the chiefs of the tribe." We are not bound by any unnatural custom like that. We must simply do our duty though it seems like plucking out a right eye, or cutting off a right arm. If we can fasten the soul to a final purpose to go straight forward in the path of goodness, whatever the opposition, that will greatly help us. "Resolved," says President Edwards, " that *I will do whatsoever* I think to be most to God's glory and my own good, ON THE WHOLE; without any consideration of the time, whether now, or never so many myriads of ages hence; to do whatever I think to be my *duty*, and most for the good and advantage of mankind in gen-

ADVANCEMENT DEMANDS EFFORT. 225

eral—whatever *difficulties* I meet with, how many and how great soever."* New life enters the soul by the mere reading of such a resolution as that.

I must so train myself that I shall not be irritated or vexed. That the things are numerous which are calculated to sour the mind, no one can doubt; but merely to flee from these things is not to flee from the native sourness of the soul. Are there persons who defame me as matter of fact? persons who slight me as matter of fact? Be it so. What follows? That I should be excited for days and weeks because of these things? Very far from it. Rather this, that I should take hold of my feelings that are apt to be rasped and put them in subjection. These feelings have no right to conquer me: I must conquer them. How is it possible to insult a man? In a vast number of cases it is the self-importance that has been insulted, and not the real man at all. Shall I then give way to my pride? This would be to unman myself; to make myself contemptible in my own eyes. A man made for immortality soured? a man

* "Works," i., p. 3.

made for the infinite God insulted? This is without meaning. What is there in the breath of a mortal, in the look of an eye that will shortly be the food of worms, in the motion of a hand that will be stiff in death quite soon? Higher up we must live. Too earthly we are. "Remember," says Epictetus, "that to the brave and wise and true there is really no such thing as misfortune; the croak of the raven can portend no harm to such a man. We do not choose our own parts in life, and have nothing to do with those parts; our simple duty is confined to playing them well. The slave may be as free as the consul; and freedom is the chief of blessings. No one can insult you if you will not regard his words or deeds as insults."

We can not very well escape from temptation, yet we may escape from the sin to which the temptation moves us. There is no causative power in temptation: it is simply the occasion of evil. The causative power lies in the bad heart and will. I shall lift a greater weight and carry a greater burden forever because I was tempted here. It is impossible for us to know the exact state of our character until we are tempted. What we deem to be favored virtues may be nothing but favored sins. "I can not praise," remarks Milton, "a fugitive and cloistered virtue, unexercised and unbreathed, that never sallies out and sees her adversary, but slinks out of the race where the immortal garland is to be run for, not without dust and heat. Assuredly we bring not innocence into the world — we bring impurity much rather; that which purifies us is trial, and trial is by what is contrary. The virtue, therefore, which is but a youngling in the contemplation of evil, and knows not the utmost that vice promises to her followers, and rejects it, is but a blank virtue, not a pure."

We are frequently told to look on the bright side, as if only in that way we can truly drill the soul in righteousness. That may be the best way to escape from trouble, but not the best way to escape from sin. No mind is a true mind that does not look on the dark as well as on the bright. To train ourselves merely to view the fair and the attractive is to cheat the soul. It is our duty to see things just as they are

I have no right to make good and evil to be less or more than they are. To look away from evil will never destroy it. The soul may sink into a pleasant reverie, but it is not redeemed in that way. The holiest men have felt sin the most: the most sinful men have felt it the least. If I would reform myself or the world, I must grasp both sin and salvation.

The religious soul should have in suitable measure the quality of moral indignation. According to the intensity of our love of goodness, should be the intensity of our hatred of wickedness. How the Saviour addressed the Scribes and Pharisees in the clear heat of his indignation! Sharply as eternal truth he tells them that they are blind guides, that they had taken away the key of knowledge, that they devoured widows' houses, that they are hypocrites, and that they could not escape the damnation of hell. The holy indignation of God has about it an infinite intensity. It is because his purity is so pure that his entire moral nature rises up against sin. The same book which affirms that "God is love," affirms that "God is a consuming fire." Human progress is only a painting of goodness, so long as a high-toned indignation is wanting. Those cycles of advance which mark the history of great souls were all commenced by a sense of sin that was deep, and a hatred of it that was holy. There are deeds of men which, the moment we see them, should awaken within us an exceedingly sharp indignation. It has been reported of the Rev. Frederick Robertson, that "he has been seen to grind his teeth, and clench his fist when passing a man who, he knew, was bent on destroying an innocent girl." There is even a punitive element in righteous indignation. It takes sides with law, demands that the guilty shall suffer.

Moral courage must also appear as the result of Christian discipline. Without this forceful quality the life will always have a certain tameness about it. Moral courage should contain the summing up of the soul's goodness; as if in this it found a way to express itself, and by this the real strength of the character was seen. It is the speech of rectitude, the voice of truth, the flame of love. The martyr Christianity is always bold. A fine specimen of boldness is presented to us by the chaplain of Frederick William the First of Prussia. The monarch was upon his dying bed; and the faithful minister addresses him in the following way. "'I have often told your majesty that Christ is the hope of our salvation, on the two conditions that we accept him with the heart, and follow his example and precepts. So long as we fail in either of these conditions, so long can we not enter into his rest. And if your majesty were to be saved by a miracle, you would not enjoy heaven, in the condition of mind in which you now are. Your army, your treasures, your lands must remain here—no courtiers can follow you there, no servants on whom you can wreak your anger. In heaven a man must have a heavenly mind.' These were words worthy of a Nathan. The king remained silent, and yet he looked round with an appealing, supplicating eye, as if to say, Will no one come to my relief? But when the attendants retired and the monarch began to recount his sins one by one, the chaplain refused to listen to so unprotestant a confession, and only demanded that the king should acknowledge the need of a change of heart, and this Frederick William would not grant. He thought that in this kings had the advantage of other men, and he insisted on justifying himself by his good works. And when some one who stood by sided with the dying man, the chaplain charged upon the poor monarch the blows which he had inflicted upon his subjects, the tyranny he had exercised over them, and the unjust sentences of death which he had passed."*

The good man must also school himself into the ministering form of Christianity. If he has gained knowledge, let him communicate that to others. If he has trained himself to logical thinking, let him use that gift in the advocacy of truth and righteousness. Has he cultivated a fine taste, so that æsthetic studies are pleasant to him? then let him imbue other minds with the same characteristic. If he has a rich and well-guarded imagination, let him yield up the treasures at his command to others; stamping the same glowing pictures upon their souls that he has in his own. Is he subjective in the cast of

---

* Haganbach, "German Rationalism," p. 21.

his mind, knowing the heights and depths that are found there? let him try and make others equally subjective, that they may understand that nature which is immortal, fallen, and lost. Is he outward in the bent of his soul, struck with that which he sees and hears? let him give all that is valuable from that quarter, whether it belongs to man or manners, to seas or stars, to insects playing in the air, or birds chanting the hymns of God. If he can make known some historical event of great moment, point to some link of a chain of Providence that is different from all others, mention a particular mountain or plain that is instinct with meaning, then let him do all this in the best way he can. If his soul has been sounded and searched by thoughts that relate to an endless life, let him make known the fact, if so be he may entice others to think of that country and kingdom where men dwell in peace forever. If the miseries of hell have startled him, so that his soul turned pale before an awful vision, then he may tell the vision to others, that they may flee from the coming wrath. Whether what he has to say be dreadful or the contrary, divine or human, let him do his duty. God is to be served whether the service brings praise or blame.

The piety of missions must also be developed. It is safe to say that the highest type of Christianity is the missionary Christianity. As specimens of pure and powerful religion, where shall we find men like Brainerd, Henry Martyn, Swartz, and Dr. Judson? What a fine class of men the Moravians have produced—humble, self-sacrificing, dying that the heathen around them might live! The missionary spirit develops a noble enthusiasm. The enthusiasm is kindled by the attempt to save the perishing. The enthusiasm clears the atmosphere of the soul, banishes doubts and fears, starts latent energies. There is holy excitement. We behold men of the burning heart. Christians should view themselves as containing a spiritual fund to be used for the eternal good of men, or at least they should view themselves as the channels through which flows the wealth of God to the nations. We are accustomed to say that a "moral sense" characterizes the whole race of man: so a *missionary sense* ought to characterize the whole race of Christians. This missionary sense should be cultivated to the highest extent possible. It should be the impersonation of divine love. If the cause of missions had done no more than lead men to give of their substance in order to send the gospel to pagan lands, it would still have done much towards purifying Christian souls. The heart is opened, refined, and expanded by this means. I am to give freely, quickly, intelligently, and largely. My gifts are to be thank-offerings and prayers. I am to keep training myself until I can give a large amount with pleasure. If I dedicate my property to God, I dedicate my soul to his service.

A leading design of the Church is to represent to the world the life of Christ. No single Christian is able to do this. One may have tenderness and courage; another, patience and perseverance; another, faith and love; another, humility and hope. When we view the collective people of God with all their graces, we catch a faint likeness of the Redeemer. The purer the Church, the loftier the Saviour appears. Men will even talk of "the sins of Jesus." when his disciples are like the common multitude. A veritable Christian is evidence that Christ is no deceiver, and Christianity no lie. If a renovating influence does flow forth from the Redeemer of men, the proof of that must be seen in a renovated Church. In Christians Christ becomes incarnate; in them he suffers and dies; in them he rises again to newness of life; and with them he ascends to the right hand of God. The cross which they carry is ever a reminder of the one on which he hung. Their tears and their travail make us to think of his agony. The love and sorrow of the entire Church of God seem to shadow forth the infinite tragedy of redemption.

CHAPTER XI.

DISCIPLINE BEST EFFECTED IN THE RELIGION OF CHRIST BY THOROUGHNESS IN ONE OR TWO THINGS.

TO a person who thinks carefully in regard to the training of the mind, a question will arise like this: Is it better to have an imperfect knowledge of many things, than a perfect knowledge of a few things? Judging by the general practice, an imperfect knowledge of many things is deemed the most desirable. Is this general practice in harmony with wisdom? Would it not be better, all things considered, to concentrate the attention upon one or two things? By adopting this method the mind is really disciplined. The discipline is continued for a sufficiently long period. This strengthens the mind. The person does not merely feel that he has thoroughly mastered one or two subjects, but along with this is the consciousness of real mental strength. He has gained the power of thinking, the power of continued abstraction. In fact he has the power to stand alone. It is not, therefore, that he knows all about one or two subjects. This is a good and desirable thing. But beyond the knowledge, he has trained himself to be a workman. The mind is educated. There is an ability to take hold of a great variety of subjects, and to go through with these in a very satisfactory and scholarly way. It is not that the person stays with the one or two subjects, as if these mark off the sum of his knowledge, and equally the amount of his mental ability. Not by any means. Having now learned the art of thinking on the one hand, and the blessedness of thoroughness on the other, he goes forward, and becomes wiser and stronger each day that he lives and each step that he takes.

Take now the other person who believes that it is best to know a little of every thing, who yet has never mastered a single subject. Why, the very first thing that strikes you in regard to this person is the fact that he has no mental training. He can not think out a difficult subject; a subject which may take days or weeks to understand. He has no inclination which would prompt him to undertake such severe mental labor. If he allowed himself to begin, he would soon grow weary. He would want to rest, and refresh himself. Then he would begin again; try for a while again; but quickly he would tire, finding that he has no mental ability for such a task. Not only is there this difficulty with a person who has a superficial knowledge of many things, but the many things which are known a little, begin very soon to fade away. They are like the seed that was sown upon stony ground which quickly sprang up, and just as quickly withered and died. There is not sufficient compass and vigor of soul to hold the multitude of little knowledges. The mind therefore, after a season, becomes meagre and empty. The mere smattering of Latin and French and history and philosophy, has vanished away, and the individual is out upon the journey of life and in the midst of the business of life with no mental capital and no mental force. Hundreds and thousands of dollars may have been spent in gaining what was thought to be a good education, but there was no education at all. The ability to think out a difficult subject has not been gained, and real knowledge approaching completeness has not been gained.

Now, the person who knows one or two things thoroughly has this advantage, that he is better able to make use of any fragmentary knowledge which he may possess, because of the vitality and depth there is to his mind. There is not that weakness about it which characterizes the individual who has swept over a great surface; and consequently the energy of soul extends over and gives life to the particles of information that have been gained. Thus the man who has mastered one or two subjects, retains these and more besides; while he who has glanced at a vast number of things, soon beholds them sinking out of his consciousness.

I have thus stated a principle relating to intellectual development, which I want to apply to religious development.

My first statement is this, that a more substantial character will be formed by mastering *one or two of the leading doctrines* of Christianity, than by simply having a slight acquaintance with very many of the doctrines. Suppose, for instance, I have gained a thorough knowledge touching the *sinful condition of human nature.* I have studied for months and years in regard to the fallen state of man, not merely from works of theology, but from the Bible, my own consciousness, and from observation. I have thus come to see how profound is the fact of sin. It sinks into the depths of the soul. Its roots I find everywhere. I perceive that there is not a faculty but that it touches. I become conscious of no sacred place in the human spirit that is free from its malign power. I notice also with what wonderful tenacity it holds its own. There is about it an enmity and determination that I, single-handed, can not overcome. I catch phase after phase of this mighty evil of souls. I am deeply impressed with what I know. I do not merely perceive intellectually that man is destitute of holiness, but I know it from conscious experience. I can truly say that by nature there dwelleth in me no good thing. I am lost; absolutely and eternally lost.

Now, such thorough acquaintance, as is nere presupposed in regard to the fallen state of man, will throw an influence over the whole sphere of Christian doctrine and life. A kind of thinking has been started and a kind of feeling has been awakened that will most certainly touch a vast variety of truths and actions. The thoroughness in regard to the fact of sin will call for a powerful and complete system of redemption. Once gain this knowledge and experience touching personal sin, and a Christian of vigorous type and serious determination will be sure to appear. Compare such a Christian with one who is superficial in the whole cast of his theology, and a difference will be seen in a moment.

Suppose, again, that having thoroughly studied the doctrine of sin, the man now thoroughly studies the nature and character of *God*, the power here will show itself very much in the same way. Let there be a clear apprehension of the divine holiness, and it will be wonderful how that will move and stimulate the soul. Not merely will one be impressed by the spotless purity of God, but this purity will react upon the soul and cause it to have a vision of its own sinfulness. Then, too, let there be a correct understanding of the divine justice and the divine mercy. These two moral attributes will not merely awaken feelings in regard to God, but they will be sure to awaken feelings with reference to the soul itself. The justice will alarm the guilty: the mercy will encourage the penitent. Indeed, if I gain a very full conception of the divine character, this will on the one hand give me an exalted conception of God, while on the other hand it will cause me to see my own littleness and sin; and then, branching out from these two conceptions, I will be led to think of the greatness and glory of the redemption of Christ. If now I am impressed by the eternity, omnipotence, and knowledge of God, a serious thoughtfulness will characterize my soul; and the truth that stands before me for acceptance will receive a coloring from my feelings.

Thus let any Christian man have a thorough acquaintance with the doctrines just stated, and it will be astonishing to see how he will go beyond all those religious persons who have not a single complete view of any truth of the divine system. The simple mastering of those thoughts that relate to God and man, seems to open up the whole scheme of life; and the slight knowledge that was possessed in regard to other things has a new freshness thrown around it: the whole being receives a quickening as if touched by the electric currents of heaven.

A second statement which I now make is this, that by *thoroughness in one or two religious states of mind* we have the best method of disciplining the soul in religion. When I look at professedly Christian people and see how variously they act in given circumstances, I can not very well explain their different courses unless I go upon the supposition that the more faithful among them have a fixed religious cast or habit of mind, while the unfaithful have nothing of that kind at all. I am very sure of this that no man will ever be a truly good man unless he has wrought into his soul what I call a religious cast or habit; a kind of pure bias that sways him, a sound consciousness that keeps him. If he is simply at the mercy of old principles of evil, broken in upon occasionally by pure thoughts and feelings, then he will have no settled drift of goodness.

Now, suppose that here is a Christian man

who has gained by repeated efforts a consciousness of that which is *infinite*. The consciousness does not merely extend over an hour or over a day, and then disappear like the sun beneath the horizon, but it remains essentially a steady consciousness of the infinite. This Christian may be taxed by his business, so that he seems to have no time to think of any thing else, yet, the very moment he rests and looks within, the consciousness of the infinite is there. The finite he knows quite well; knows how meagre and empty it is. It meets not the wants of an immortal spirit. As well feed a hungry man with sand, as a God-created soul with that which passes away. Millions, however, live, and millions die, having never found any thing else than that which is limited. But the Christian that we are thinking about has entered into the region of the infinite. He lives in view of unbounded realities. He drinks at eternal fountains. The sun that illumines his being never sets, and the air that he breathes is the air of God. He may tarry here as other men tarry, work here as other men work, smile and weep as other men smile and weep; yet the cast of his mind turns that mind to another sphere; he communes with the infinite, feels at home there, is blessed there. This sense of the infinite modifies all this man's life. It touches and turns the smallest action as well as the greatest. A great magnet seems to draw him onward. Now, I say, with this sense of the infinite quite complete, although it be but one phase of the mind, it really commands that mind, gives wonderful meaning to it, makes the man to feel that he is a stranger among friends, that his native land is not here, that his brothers and sisters live in the city of God, and that only in that region of life will he be at rest, with purity that has no stain. Far different from this man is the other one who is in what may be called a state of religious mediocrity. The commonplace runs through all. There is a field with grass and flowers, but every thing is stinted. No streams run through it to give it life. The dew of night only falls upon it. Not like the garden of God does it seem, although God may walk through it. There is no tree of life with fruit and singing birds; no bower of bliss where the angels sit down at noon. It is a dry and weary place Death and life are struggling. Heaven is not near.

Let us imagine now that the religious man has a deep *consciousness of salvation*. Each moment of life he feels the need of this salvation, and each moment of life he applies it to his heart. There is no business so pressing as to make him forget it, and no cares so annoying as to make him lose sight of it. He works his way through life with a steady eye fixed on the great redemption; feeling that time is nothing without it, and that eternity is all because of it. He is no legalist drilling himself as best he can; straining the faculties that sin may sicken and die; lashing the passions that they be still; polishing the conscience that it may be clear; spurring the will that it may rush into obedience. No doubt he works hard and works long, but all his power comes from Christ. His whole character may be called redemptive. He breathes the air of Calvary; rays from the cross illuminate his soul; the Crucified One inspires him; he is washed in the blood of the Lamb. His disposition may be called Christly, and his life through all the hours is a Christly life. With this consciousness of salvation the discipline of the soul is healthy. The method instead of being circuitous, is direct; instead of being manifold, it is single; instead of being natural, it is supernatural. In this way there is no waste. Power is not scattered and weakened: it is economized and concentrated.

Again, *complete self-forgetfulness* is the surest way to reach completeness of character. There may be prejudices and passions in our nature that seek to be gratified, a strong disinclination to suffer, a number of thorny characteristics which bristle out at the trumpet call of duty, and so half heartedly we enter upon the work of holiness. Egoism stands ever in our way, and we accomplish but little. The orator is never himself till he loses sight of himself. The poet is never a poet until he is carried away from himself by a great inspiration. The scholar will never accomplish any thing unless he has the power of abstraction. "In a military expedition which Socrates made along with Alcibiades, the philosopher was seen by the Athenian army to stand for a whole day and a night, until the breaking of the second morning, motionless, with a fixed gaze,— thus showing that he was uninterruptedly engrossed with the consideration of a single object." We only seem to live when we are lost in truth, lost in holiness, lost in God. To be perpetually thinking of self is an utter degradation. Why can not I live in the midst of a benevolent passion, seeking only the good of the men who are about me? Am I not in bondage just to the extent that I think of myself? The misery we suffer on the one hand, and the happiness we crave on the other, seem to call forth a great deal of self-consciousness. We are troubled in regard to what men think of us. Their praises we value too highly: their frowns we fear too much. Would it not be an infinite gain to escape from self for a single day? Would it not be happiness itself to concentrate our powers upon a single immortal soul, trying to rescue that soul from eternal sin and eternal death? Are there not wondrous thoughts so far-reaching and valuable, that I ought to lose myself in their golden radiance, and by that very means be transfigured? Can not I have a sentiment for the divine so all embracing, that my individual self shall sink out of sight by reason of the greatness of the Divine Object? What nobility can there be to a soul that is perpetually occupied about its own little affairs, forgetful of that immensity of existence that is all around? Is there no exalted mission in the universe of God that may call forth the energies of the human spirit, sinking by the very intensity of the actions all concern of that spirit for itself? Was it not the meat and drink of Christ to do his Father's will? Is it not said of him that he "pleased not himself"? Surely the way to discipline the soul in piety, is to reach forth to the attainment of self-abnegation. If it be a fact that I am in Christ and am to be saved by him alone, then my business is to live for him. I am to remember the Redeemer, and forget myself. I can not think of him too much, nor think of myself too little. If God and heaven be mine, then I may work with the utmost self-forgetfulness.

But is not this very self-forgetfulness a difficult state to reach? It is. There is nothing great in souls or out of them that is reached with ease. Sin only is easy, yet it is not easy. By the touch of a match a ball will be sent off from a cannon, but not by a mere volition will a man be driven away from himself. Self-forgetfulness is an art, as well as a holy state of mind, and we must keep trying to practice it till the art is learned. If mental abstraction can be cultivated, so can moral. We do not enter upon the service of God with sufficient purpose. Eternal obligations do not press down upon us. We allow ourselves too much freedom; and so we sin without much pain, and find holiness without much joy. If we set the mind upon the business in hand and hold it there for an hour, we shall be all the stronger for the hour's effort. Why may we not fix a habit of holy attention, as well as a habit of self-attention? Our life is too hap-hazard, too much a matter of course. We do not bind ourselves down to duty, determined to act as commanded.

When I open my Bible and look through it, I do find statements relating to a great variety of duties; yet I find also the compact and condensed method of drilling the soul through governing states of mind. I notice, for instance, that God is made the centre, and that whether I eat, or drink, or whatsoever I do, all must be done to his glory. What is this but calling into play a great generic thought, feeling, and purpose? Then, again, how faith is emphasized; making the whole Christian life to be connected with it; so that the life rises or falls, as the faith is strong or weak. More can be done for the discipline of the soul by *perfecting faith* than by fixing our attention on thousands of minute acts. In all false religions the mind is made to follow after a round of services,—many prayers, offerings, penances, fastings, and works,—all exactly specified as a merchant marks his goods in his store. This is being religious by a kind of spiritual arithmetic: the only way that man has struck upon when left to himself. The Bible method, while it never loses sight of the smallest actions, points to leading movements of soul as of the first importance, because by these the whole man is controlled. Let there be a profound sense of obligation, a state of pure love, a penitential frame of mind, or any other spiritual habits, and the work is done.

John Gerson, the Reformer before the Reformation, was a man of great parts and great humility. On the day before his death he called the little children together whom he had been accustomed to teach, and requested them to offer up this prayer for him when he was gone: "O God, my Creator, have mercy on thy poor servant, John Gerson." Not even satisfied with this, he directed that there should be carved on his tombstone the words: "Pray for poor John Gerson." However unsound this may be in doctrine, it shows that the *state of unworthiness* was a leading power in the formation of his character. The likeness of Calvin, as seen in the old editions of his works, has under it this motto—"*Prompte et sincere*"—*Promptly* and *honestly*. Here, again, there is a call for leading moral habits. He who has a soldier-like promptness, ready for action at any moment, with a heart that is honest in the sight of God—such an one will be able to train himself in all good things. "When Grotius was dying, he was asked what he would recommend to others. He replied, '*Be serious, be serious.*'" This distinguished man knew that seriousness was an important state of mind, that it was a kind of spiritual atmosphere surrounding the soul, and so, by having this, a great deal would follow from it that is good and true. On Herder's monument at Weimar were inscribed the words—"*Light, love, life.*" Such language implies a luminous state for the intellect, and a loving and living state for the affections and will.

CHAPTER XII.

NON-VOLUNTARY INFLUENCE AS AFFECTING THE RELIGION OF CHRIST.

IN this age of assertion and positive effort, many are apt to think that there is no way to form character save by direct means. This is a great mistake. It is a question whether non-voluntary influence is not as powerful as the influence that is voluntary. "We are told that the tone of a bell depends in part upon the imperceptible vibrations of the atmosphere, when, in the moments of fusion, the metal is settling in the mould. So is it with a Christian character. Powers unknown and unthought of, and circumstances soon and long forgotten, and occasions scarcely observed in their passing, may give to it that tone which can not be described and the cause of which can not be defined, and yet which shall distinguish it forever." Influence is a very mysterious agent; working many a time in a very mysterious way. It seems to be a kind of invisible power, set to work by the Creator at the occupation of fashioning souls.

If we look at *nature*, simply acting in its own sphere, we can see that it is ever sending forth an influence. Take the *ocean* that spans the globe; viewing it not merely in the abstract as a body of water. It is the source of vapor; that vapor ascends; it moves round the globe in its airy chariot; it descends to the earth in the form of rain: the life of man and beast depends upon it. Look at the *air* also that surrounds the earth. It is a great invisible sea many miles deep. The clouds like ships of God sail through it; like celestial islands they float over it. The air is the great lung of the earth; the lung that is filled with constant life; the lung that heaves with every moment of time. We all live because of this ocean of air that is ever about us. Its very fineness seems to show the fineness of life. It is a great unseen power, just as life is a great unseen energy. Take *light*; what an ethereal universe that is! It seems like the empire of spirits; like the garment of God; like the radiance that streams forth from the Eternal. How gently that light settles down upon us. It wakes not the infant out of its slumber; it reaches the small eye of the insect with a smile; its footsteps are like those of the angels when they pass through among us. Take away that light, and we should have nothing but death. Look at *gravitation*; how sweeping that is! It connects itself with all systems. Each atom of matter feels its power. It is the silent servant of God; the obedient messenger of the Supreme. That messenger comes to us all; keeps us where we are; holds us by a power from which we can not escape.

How *we ourselves are influenced by scenes of nature.* What power there is in a landscape! The lofty mountains stretching far away; the valleys and green fields; the solemn forest of trees; the winding streams; the men at work, and the cattle feeding on the plain; the distant village with its curling smoke; the church spire pointing to heaven; the railway train dashing past; the birds gliding through the air; the children returning from school,—such a landscape impresses the soul; a strange power comes over us; we stand and look around, or sit down that we may be refreshed. The flower with its sweet perfume, and the bee that hums in its journey of pleasant toil, influence us. Then when we turn our eyes to the glorious sunrise or the glorious sunset, we seem to think that heaven's palace gates are opened, and that the chiefs of eternity are coming forth that they may spend an hour in wandering through the skies of time. Angels seem to be all about us. They are sitting in the clouds and in the sun. They fly past, or walk, or stand still, as the case may be. They smile upon us in the hour of peace; their heavenly eye rests upon us in the hour of sadness; they point upward to the great kingdom of eternal joy.

Suppose we are standing by the shore of the sea, and looking off upon that great presence. What an influence reaches us! We behold the billows as they foam and break asunder. We hear them dash against the rocks. The waves roll up upon the beach, and echo as they roll. That sea is an image of the race. It speaks to us all. It tells us what we are. When it is at rest, and no wind sweeps it, it tells us of fairer climes and a serene land. Is it night, and we are looking forth into the darkness? We view the eternal stars as they sparkle amidst the immense obscurity. There is silence all about us. Our spirit is awed. Longings that go beyond the stars, that enter into the region of the eternities, arise in our God-created souls. We stay not here. Our bodies only are here. Our immortal spirits spread their wings as if to reach an infinite realm. The sound of a waterfall as it strikes the ear amidst the silence of our being; a solitary tree standing after all the other trees have been cut down; a moss-covered ruin; a cave long and dark; the wail of the midnight wind; a fall of snow,—these all influence the soul. Nature awakens our emotions far more than we know.

But we will turn our attention to the *human* side of things, that we may see how non-voluntary influence affects us from that quarter. Take the fact of *temperament* to begin with. I suppose there are minds that are really approaching the Eternal Light, who yet have about them a strange heaviness. They seem to be carrying a burden, trembling and staggering under the weight that bears them down. These persons are aiming to reach heaven under great disadvantages. The remedy of Christ never exerts its full power in their soul. It is compelled to work in a crooked and circuitous manner,—never going straight to the centre of evil and laying it low. In the midst of a mysterious sorrow, these children of the evening wander through the years; hoping in Christ, yet afraid to hope; believing, yet always doubting. They are puzzled and perplexed in regard to their spiritual condition. Who can fail to see that the piety of John Foster received a coloring from his melancholy temperament. He dwelt in the midst of the twilight; the full-orbed sun never shining down upon him. Professor B. B. Edwards, a man of fine scholarship, taste, and piety, yet self-distrustful, pensive, and marching on to the Infinite Blessedness hampered by a hidden pain. In the common walks of Christianity, many a lonely spirit is working its way towards the great life, crippled and shaded by an unfavorable temperament. There are silent souls, who hide their griefs, who toil and travel through their night of probation, not knowing but that they may reach the day of God at last. Herodotus mentions "a stream which is lukewarm at early dawn; at the time when the market fills it is much cooler; by noon it has grown quite cold; at this time, therefore, they water their gardens. As the afternoon advances, the cold goes off, till, about sunset, the water is once more lukewarm; still the heat increases, and at midnight it boils furiously. After this time it again begins to cool, and grows less and less hot till morning comes. This spring is called '*the Fountain of the Sun.*'"* The sombre and depressed followers of Christ need just such a fountain in their heart, that with it they may be warmed and comforted during their cold night of exile.

There is another class of pious men, however, who are favored with a temperament of hope and gladness. These, as compared with the kind just mentioned, have a stronger faith, a lovelier love, and a view of life and man that is more cheerful. They seem to be making a fine passage to the King's land. They appear to us as heavenly vessels sailing over the sea of

* Rawlinson's "Herodotus," vol. iii., p. 131.

peace, the soft winds bearing them onward, and angelic pilots steering them safely towards the eternal ports of life. There is a certain attraction about such Christians. They make pleasant companions, joyful laborers, encouraging speakers. "Hopeful," in the "Pilgrim's Progress," belonged to this class. He could see the city of God, while Christian could not. "He had much ado to keep his brother's head above water; yea, sometimes he would be quite gone down, and then, ere a while, he would rise up again half dead. Hopeful did also endeavor to comfort him, saying, 'Brother, I see the gate and the men standing by to receive us'; but Christian would answer, 'It is you, it is you they wait for; for you have been hopeful ever since I knew you.'" It is fair to believe that many a death-bed experience has been clouded, because of a temperament that was sad; and many a death-bed experience has been clear, because of a temperament that was struck upon the key of joy. There are Christians of great force and activity, and Christians who are backward and sluggish—each class touched and turned somewhat by temperament. The sanguine and the cautious are moved upon by different influences. The brain of one man predominates, and he needs exercise and society. The heart of another man is too active, and he needs rest. Another man still is phlegmatic, and he needs excitement.

It would seem almost as if there were a kind of *national* temperament; as if a whole people were modified by that strange power. When we look at the different Christian nations, we can see that the piety of one differs from the piety of another. One people has feeling in their religion, while another has thought; one has form, while another has freedom; one has self-denial and sternness, while another has pleasure and elasticity. It seems almost as if there were a kind of *physical* temperament to the land where each people dwells; as if the land itself were a man; a man of mundane qualities; and influencing souls in a way that is peculiar. We naturally think that a country with mountains is conducive to human liberty. A land, the chief part of which is bounded by the ocean, will prompt to trade and commerce.

Leaving the temperaments and coming to the appetite of *hunger*, it is truly wonderful how that single appetite has influenced the soul at every point. The intellect, the conscience, the heart, the will, are all modified by that sense of hunger which has been placed in the body. A certain character has been stamped upon religion by this strange power. The very poor and the very rich are not usually distinguished for great piety. It is the middle class who have advanced Christianity in the world. It would seem as if the religion of men with their appetite of hunger, and the religion of the angels without that appetite, must differ in some respects from each other. "Hunger is the most powerful stimulus to activity, and hence to the development of the spirit, and ever since the entrance of sin into the race, there has been no other so sure and effectual a means of stirring up the spirit out of its slothful indolence. In the present state of man hunger is not only of significance for the individual; it is a world-historical power, the first and most persistent stimulus to civilization."*

* Wuttke, "Christian Ethics," vol. ii., p. 66.

A human *countenance* of a certain kind may influence us for good. The character may be epitomized in the features. These features may be eloquent with love and faithfulness, and so they may impress us with great power. We are looking at a picture, one of the pictures of God, and divine thoughts reach us from every part of it. Celestial influences steal into the heart, and fashion it in a way peculiar to themselves. We are very often awed by a human presence; rendered serious by it; brought to a complete stand by its magic power. The silent ministry of the eye may awaken in us emotions of grief, pity, and courage.

The Bacchiadae, who at one time were the governing race in Corinth, ordered ten persons to go and put to death the infant child of Aëtion. "The men went to Petra, and entered into Aëtion's house, and there asked if they might see the child; and Labda, who knew nothing of their purpose, but thought their inquiries arose from a kindly feeling towards her husband, brought the child, and laid him in the arms of one of them. Now they had agreed by the way that whoever first got hold of the child should dash it against the ground. It happened, however, by a providential chance, that the babe, just as Labda put him into the man's arms, *smiled* in his face. The man saw the smile, and was touched with pity, so that he could not kill it; he therefore passed it on to his next neighbor, who gave it to a third; and so it went through all the ten without any one choosing to be the murderer. The mother received her child back, and the men went out of the house, and stood near the door, and there blamed and reproached one another; chiefly however accusing the man who had first had the child in his arms, because he had not done as had been agreed upon."* Surely here is a fine instance of non-voluntary influence. Rough men were hindered from carrying out a murderous plan by the *smile* of a helpless infant. Many a time souls are checked and changed by agencies which, in themselves, seem to have no value.

There is a *passive* side in religion which affects us favorably. Here is a pious man who is weak, sickly, absolutely poor, and confined at home; yet what an influence he

* Rawlinson's "Herodotus," vol., iii., p. 244.

sends forth! Mark his submission: no complaint is ever heard. He feels that he is in the hands of Perfect Wisdom. Contentment is the atmosphere he breathes. Peace is enthroned in his spirit. Humility clothes him with a garment like to that of the angels. Gentleness gives character to his whole being. Reverence solemnizes his soul. Hope causes him to be radiant with the glories of heaven. This person does but little, says but little; yet how much of holy influence streams forth from him! His character, taken in its totality, is a great power: virtue goes out from it. He is a representative of spiritual life, and that life travels forth on its mission of love.

Religion also is shaped by *laws of association*. One man looks to form, color, and circumstance; and so his religion is literal, outward, and showy. Another man looks to cause and effect; and his type of piety is substantial and sanctifying. Another person fastens his eye on time and place; and he is exact and somewhat artificial. Another person still is affected by resemblances; and he is imitative and superficial. The more we penetrate into the spiritual realm, making our home in the midst of the divine, our laws of association will be finer, and the character which they form will be more finished. It was the remark of a painter that no one could draw a tree, unless in some sense he became a tree. It will be very difficult for us to fashion the soul in highest purity, if suggestions are crawling over us from surrounding wickedness; whilst on the other hand, if our abode is with the Son of God we are transformed into his likeness.

See how non-voluntary influence works around a good *home*. This is really the moulding power in families. It is not merely the direct effort that is put forth to benefit the young, not the rules that are laid down with great care, not the threatening and the penalty; but it is the *spiritual atmosphere* of the household which chiefly forms character. There is a life which comes from the collective moral forces of the parents, and that life touches the heart and conscience of the children. The very tone of the voice, the way of doing things, influence the mind. There is *law* in such a family; but how does it work? The law is a presence, and each child is awed by it, governed by it, and made what it ought to be by it. This reign of law is like a sun shining forever; its golden light always there, in the midst of which one may walk; growing always with each moment and day as children of light; the understanding and character pure as the light. Living thus, the child is bathed as in a celestial fountain. It advances towards heaven as if guardian angels were ever around it. There need not be any thing rough or fierce about law. It may be like the dew that falls upon the flower; like the music that falls upon the ear; like the light that falls upon the eye. The law may seem like a hymn of the angels, chanted along the days of life; a law made of love, covered with the white robes of purity; a queen of righteousness throned in the homes of men, ruling over them with a sceptre of peace.

Many a soul is also polished and purified by submitting to the painful ministry of *trouble*. "Old travellers mention a wondrous eastern tree, which by daylight stands leafless and flowerless, but after sun-down puts forth countless white blossoms, shining in the darkness like the drops of a silver fountain." During the dark hours of life we are to be clothed with beauty like that strange tree. There are afflictions which startle the spirit of man, search it, render it thoughtful, make it humble. They affect all the emotions,—the earthly, the moral, and the religious. They strike the understanding, the reason, the imagination, and the memory. They put in motion aspirations that were dull, and cause them to leap towards unbounded realities. They touch the soul at its centre, and call forth into the light images that were wandering through darkened halls and sub-conscious chambers. "In the Black Forest lies a lake, bordered deep with lilies. As the traveller gazes on that white waving margin of the dark waters, he is told that those lilies, on the last moonlighted midnight, assumed their spirit-forms,—were white-robed maidens, dancing on the mere; till at a warning voice, they resumed, ere daybreak, the shape of flowers." Around every lake of bitterness are found beautiful lilies. During the night of trial they are transformed into angels of comfort. A legend says that when Eve had broken the divine command "she wept bitterly; and her tears, which flowed into the ocean, were changed into costly pearls, while those which fell on the earth brought forth all beautiful flowers." A chastened penitence is always followed by pearls and flowers. There are souls that sleep till a great sorrow awakes them. The night blooming cereus, after a long growth, sends forth its flower at night, closing it before sunrise. So some men, after years of hidden development, bloom forth in the darkness, and that but once. They speak their word, or perform their act, and then depart. Their noblest work was done during the hour of affliction. They flourish, and then fall; shine, and sink to be seen not again.

What an influence comes to us from *death* —the death of a friend! Here there is no life, no action, the soul even is gone, the dead body is all that remains; and yet there is influence. As we look at the pale face, the eyes closed forever, the lips that utter no sound, there is influence. Why do we imprint the kiss on the cold cheek, and drop the tear on the lifeless body, if there is no influence? Yes, there is an influence that is tender and touching: life seems to come from death. The influence of an infant that stays with us a few days, and then dies, is even very great. The young stranger never spoke to us while here. It lived to a great extent a hidden life. It just began to smile, began to detect a particular voice, and then it died. A world of emotion, however, it has awakened in the soul. Sleeping in its little coffin, it seems more precious than when it slept in its little cradle. Its death is a far greater event than was its birth. Many voices echo out of its silence; and the darkness of death leads the mind away to a light that is shining in a far-off land. In passing through a forest, your attention may be arrested by a beautiful tree, sending forth many branches, the whole finely proportioned; and at the foot of it a little flower may be seen, nestling close up beside it as it were for protection. A terrible gale strikes the tree, and overturns it and the flower together. They both lie withered in the dust. So have I seen a mother and her infant fall by the hand of death. They were both placed in the same coffin, laid in the same grave, to sleep there till the morning of the last great day.

O Death! how thou hast affected men. How many hearts thou hast broken! Thou hast no compassion. Thy nature is of steel, cold and sharp. We can not plead with thee; can use no bribe; tears soften thee not. All men fear thee. Thou art "the king of terrors." How we shrink from thine approach! We know not what thou art. Not till thy icy hand is laid upon us shall we understand thee. We have conversed with no one who has entered thine iron gate, who has looked into eternity, and who has come back to us again with tidings of the viewless land. One by one, sad and anxious, the whole race must follow thee. There are men who assume to care not for thee. They are brave in their madness. When thy shadow falls upon them, they will be seized with an inward trembling. It is not, O Death, that thou art going to take the soul out of the body which so alarms us, but it is the dread possibility that we may be doomed forever. Shall I be lost, or saved? Prepared or unprepared, I must go when thou comest. In the very midst of a prayer thou wilt seize me. In life I must be ready for thee. In Christ I am safe.

To the pious man thou art simply the dark entrance that leads to the palace of God.

What an influence reaches us as we walk through a *graveyard*; especially a graveyard where our acquaintances and friends are sleeping till the last great day. We stand before one grave after another; see the flowers that have been planted there by the hand of affection; read the words on the tombstones: an influence steals into the soul, into the heart, into the most sacred place of the heart. All the various styles of symbolism—the broken pillar, the cross, the crown—impress us. Here is the sculptured figure of a man with one hand resting upon the stock of an anchor, and the other pointing to heaven—we are reminded of faith and hope. Even the grave that is marked by no memento of any kind, affects us. All over the silent city of the dead there are voices eloquent with life and with love; voices that speak to the soul, conversing with the emotions, and with the sighs that wander away.

Non-voluntary influence springs from the *inevitable*. However much we may glorify freedom, and however thankful we may be that we are characterized by it, there is yet a great realm that is stamped with necessity. Events are occurring day by day which are entirely beyond our range of power. We see them rolling over the sea of time like waves; as winds they sweep in all directions; as meteoric stones they fly through our atmosphere. There are providential movements that we can not control. They come upon us without our choice. We speak of fate as having no existence, and yet it holds us fast. We are bounded on every hand. We can not extend life so as to match with our desires. When the moment comes it ends. Weakness and frailty can not be banished from the earth. There is no eternal youth here; no gladsome joys that have no grief; no summer loves without their winter of care. There is a *nemesis* along our path. A deity of retribution meets us. We are in the midst of a moral system, and out of it we can not escape. There are phases of character that seem like nature itself: habits of sin fixed as eternity; habits of holiness that sway the mind forever like the rulers of God. How inevitable also is the soul itself. It never can die. The most unhappy spirit can not annihilate itself. Live we must forever and ever; and live just where character places us. What wondrous influences fall upon us from the inevitable realm!

If we lift our eyes and view the whole world of man, trying to realize the exact state of things upon this earth, it is evident that a great river of non-voluntary influence is moving around the globe every instant of time, and equally evident that not one person in a thousand thinks of this astonishing fact. When all the individual wills have spent their force upon their multitude of acts, there is away beyond these acts a power that has resulted from them, and that power is non-voluntary in its nature. Influences are moving round us from all quarters, yet we can not marshal off these influences into separate lines, and trace them back to distinct human wills. We are simply in the midst of exceedingly fine potencies, but whence they come and whither they go, we can not tell. All we know is, that, in a number of cases, non-voluntary influence is a remote descendant of that which was voluntary,—power is travelling long after the will has left it, and that isolated and fragmentary power is working upon souls in a way that is mysterious.

Here, for instance, is a literature that has been formed by the mind of man. That literature, apart from the reading of it, and simply by its existence, is sending forth an influence. The mere fact that I know that such an amount of mental force is embodied in millions of volumes, is a power that touches my spiritual nature. I feel as if my consciousness were greatly extended by the mere existence of such untold wealth. The impression which I gain is not simply from the few pages which I read in the course of a lifetime: I am affected by the simple magnitude of the literature itself. Here, again, is a body that we call the Christian Church. An influence goes out from this Christian Church entirely separate from the volitions of its different members. Viewed simply as a commonwealth of pious men, it is impressing minds and hearts the world over. Even those who have never looked upon this divine-human kingdom, but have learned of its existence, are influenced as a matter of fact. The indirect power of Christianity in a world like this, is immense. It reaches us many a time when we know it not; making us to feel fresher than we were before, and sending thoughts through our minds that lead us to heaven. It seems almost as if, at times, there were spiritual influences in the air. We are solemnized as by some hidden power, and walk softly as if on the borders of the unknown land.

And then when we think of Christ during the long centuries since he left us, it seems as if he were still here. Surely his shadow is walking through all the earth, and the echo of his voice lingers with us through all the years. In the busy crowd or in the deep seclusion of our being he seems to be at our side, uttering words of peace, or tracking his way to the world from which he came. In the night of our weeping he scatters the darkness and the grief; filling our cup from the golden goblet of his love; leaving benedictions to gladden us when he is gone. There is life in all our dwellings and along the great wastes of the sea that has come from him. We enter no region where his power is not felt. The perfume of his seamless robe lingers with us all, and our steps are the faster because he has travelled the same way before us. The breezes of heaven seem to have been fanning our fevered souls ever since he left us, and the radiance of God has never departed from our sky during all the time he has been away.

Christ and Christianity are thoughts, powers, pictures. They face man as beauty does; enter into him as life enters; smile upon him as the sun the trees of winter. There is no excellence that is brighter than they are, nor any joy that equals their gladness. Our infinite aspirations and wants, our sins and our sadness, find in them worlds of relief. They surely come to us from above, as if the glory of beginningless ages were about them; their speech the language of Eternal Goodness, uttered to hearts that have no peace. The silk-worm and the seraph, the flower and the star, seem to be images of their heavenly power.

CHAPTER XIII.

CONCEALED GREATNESS AN ADVANCED PHASE OF THE RELIGION OF CHRIST.

THERE are three grades of pious men: the inferior, the medium, and the superior. The *inferior* class are struck with feebleness. The piety seems as if it were diseased; seems as if it were consumptive. This low type of spiritual life is like the low type of bodily life that we sometimes witness. Here is a person who is not able to walk; the nervous energy is gone; there is no appetite. Sometimes a child is born in such a state of weakness that it is doubtful whether it can live. It lives, however, for years; but that is all. There are Christians who seem to be just alive, and no more. They are a kind of religious zoöphites.

The *medium* class of pious men are those who illustrate the common Christianity of the day. This form of life is mixed. There is spirituality and worldliness, benevolence and selfishness, humility and pride, faith and unbelief, love and hatred, hope and fear, watchfulness and carefulness, Sabbath keeping and Sabbath breaking, temperance and intemperance, courage and cowardice. The natural man fixing his eye on the dark features of this religion is led to doubt. We condemn all that is bad about it. Sin can not be justified. Still we must admit that there is goodness—only the goodness is imperfect. The medium Christian is not by any means satisfied with himself; he is somewhat ashamed; and yet, it must be confessed, he does not become much better. At the end of forty or fifty years we very frequently see the same inconsistent being. Sin must be a terrible evil, that it thus holds and hampers souls.

The *superior* class of pious men are the select few. They are the men of concealed greatness. The words that follow will point them out.

"The theory of signatures proceeded on the supposition that every creature bears, in some part of its structure or outward conformation, the indication of the character or virtue inherent in it—the representation, in fact, of its idea or soul." This is almost a fancy. There are men, for instance, who have a greater amount of *intellectual* power than they seem to have. No index points out their mental ability. A treasure is hidden in the soul which no creature beholds. We can not tell what they are by a first acquaintance. Not even by an acquaintance that extends over months can we understand them. They have no inclination to dazzle, to astonish, to overpower; they may dazzle, may astonish, may overpower; but to try to do these things is not in harmony with their minds. Inferior characters will generally make the most ado. There are too many wise men without wisdom, too many good men without goodness, too many great men without greatness. It is the characteristic of a small mind to appear greater than it is, while it is the characteristic of a great mind to appear smaller than it is. A well-endowed human spirit has compass and depth. It spreads over years, detects causes, searches for principles. There are persons who have such a reach of thought, and the thought is so fine and ethereal, that only a favored few can perceive it. They are working out towards a region that is seldom visited; are bordering upon a sphere which, to a common mind, is the same as absolute nothingness. There is a species of intuition in some souls, a certain divineness, as if a very bright spark of the Infinite were illuminating their being, and they were shut off in a kind of royal seclusion like stars in a new sky. Persons have appeared who were ahead of their age, and who consequently were not known when they lived. In fact many a jewel is not discovered until it is washed upon the shores of eternity. Only the light that is everlasting can point it out.

There are a number of things that may cast a veil over mental greatness. The very looks of the person may be against him. The body is not attractive. Thought is not seen in the countenance. The eye is not expressive. The forehead is not what is called intellectual. The sound of the voice is harsh, and not fitted to express fine emotions. The words may also be at fault. The style may not have been sufficiently cultivated. Then the individual may have a certain awkwardness. A native bashfulness may have run to an extreme. The manner is not at all pleasing. In addition to these, there may be ill health and poverty. By such means the soul is in a state of eclipse. The real man is not seen. It would not be strange if he should sink in his own estimation, as well as sink in the estimation of others.

There are men who have a deeper flow of piety than they appear to have. You may mingle with a hundred individuals during a single day, and it may be difficult to tell in what respect they differ morally, though there is, in fact, a vast difference between them. Many things are not visibly changed by the possession of piety. You behold the thoroughly Christian man attending to his business, very much as another man is attending to his who is not a Christian. One works as hard as the other, as long as the other, as well as the other. In buying and selling there may be no perceptible difference between them. Profits and prices may be very much alike. The rise and fall of the market, the principles of commercial justice, a certain business judgment, may influence each one in the same way; so that you can not very well distinguish the religious man from the one who is not religious. The converted man has to pay his debts in the same way that the unconverted man has to pay his; simple honesty belongs to both. There is a great deal of conversation also that must be carried forward on the same level; so that to hear a Christian talk in certain circumstances, is just like hearing one talk who is not a Christian. When a man becomes a follower of Christ, there must be many things which, to the outward eye, seem to be done in the same way that they were formerly done. The regenerated man salutes you just as he has done for years; says good evening or good morning with the same tone of voice. He speaks of the weather as hot or cold, cloudy or clear, pleasant or unpleasant, as he has always done. He wears clothes, eats food, lives in a house, sleeps, visits friends, as he did before he thought any thing about religion. The superficial critic may say that Christianity is a mere name, for the man who professes to believe in it is just like other men. Like other men he is, in many respects. This we wish understood. For the want of understanding a fact so plain, there is great confusion. Religion does not transform a human being into an angel. We can not always tell a Christian the moment we see him, just as we can not always tell a poet or philosopher the moment we see him. I do not know but that persons carry about with them the thought that if they can not recognize a Christian at once, then there is nothing in Christianity. They evidently want to see some wonderful being, a kind of second Adam, a perfect man; and because they see no such personage they are disappointed. "Show us a sign from heaven and we will believe," is their demand. We have no sign of that kind.

Let it be distinctly known that the Christian is a veritable man. He struggles and weeps, is afflicted and suffers, just like millions of other men. That there is a curative element in his soul, we fully believe; that that curative element will one day come off triumphant, we can not deny; but the remedy is out of sight, and the totality of its effects can not be seen by looking on the outside. That there is an outward sphere where religion *does* show itself, we admit. The test, that "by their fruits ye shall know them," we fully accept. The true

Christian *is* faithful in all the duties of life. His sound judgment makes him to act wisely; his sound conscience makes him to act justly; his sound heart makes him to act lovingly. There is a vast range of duty to which he attends. Every faculty and every principle of action are stronger. There are not so many crosses to be carried. Habits of holiness have been formed; and so there is a kind of divine ease and pleasantness in acting them out. The outward life viewed from a human stand-point, is to a great extent blameless. Speech is well-guarded; a noble truthfulness touches every thing; obedience has become somewhat natural. Instead of being unable to do good, the person finds himself unable to do evil. Apart, however, from objective goodness, there is a subjective realm where spiritual character is in process of formation; and although the eye of sense can not see the greatness of the work that is going on there, yet it is just as certain as the building up of coral reefs in the depths of ocean. "The kingdom of God cometh not with observation." One can not say, "Lo here! or, lo there! the kingdom of God is within you."

"What any one *means*," says Dr. Whichcote, "is rather his action than what he does; for in what he *means* he hath absolute power, it is wholly his own; in what a man doth, he may be liable to engagements and force. Therefore we say the mind of a good man is the best part of him, and the mind of a bad man is the worst part of him; because the one hath more good in his heart than he can perform; the other more evil in his heart than he can execute."* The *inward* Christian is not to be judged by principles of sensationalism. Sound does not sound him. Silence many a time is a better exponent of his character. He acts as well as others, speaks as well as others; but aside from outward activity however good, there is a world of piety that can not be seen. We know nothing of the heart-repentings, the inward struggles that are put forth to gain the victory over self, the longing for the pure and the divine. There is frequently a delicacy of soul that we are not aware of,—the outward symbolism of life not being sufficient to set it forth. What do we know, by merely looking at the outside, of that fine

* "Aphorisms," p. 251.

taste for holiness,—the soul alive to the least touch of sin, and the utter pain and grief when sin has been committed? You can behold the sun and the clouds, the waving trees and passing men, reflected on the face of a stream; but the great world of emotion does not show its image in the eye, or paint its likeness on the countenance. How can I tell, by looking at a human being, of those aspirations that travel around the universe, that run far upward to the throne of God, that centre themselves on him who sits upon that throne? The strong faith that has no wavering is an invisible reality, and the bright hope which beckons the spirit away to its rest is the hidden angel of the heart. There are fine spirits whose goodness is shaded by a cloud of sorrow. They pass through life, and are never seen as they are. They leave us, only to be known in a better land. The Lord has many hidden ones in a world like this. He sees them where wicked men see them not. Passed aside they may be; despised and put to death they may be; but they are sons of God none the less. There are streams of benevolence which bless many a soul; but whose source no one ever beholds. There are plans of goodness so divine, that frigid people pronounce them to be unwise. There is an exactness in duty which receives the name of contractedness, and an attachment to principle so unwavering that the person who manifests it is called stubborn.

We are not sufficiently subjective in our estimates of character. Currents of life may be flowing through the soul, which to us are unknown; but not unknown to God. These currents of life may turn many a wheel of power, ending in great blessings to men. They may start trains of thought of infinite value; produce emotion that may give character and point to a whole discourse; develop a spiritual tendency that may not be lost for years; inspire a course of action that may tell upon the destiny of thousands. The course of action which comes to the light may be all that we see, and we may found our judgment altogether upon that; but in the depths of the soul the chief power has been at work, and no human eye beholds it. Only the Divine Being can truly estimate character, because all that is inward and all that is outward stands present to his view. There is no man who has done a great work for the race but who has had his hours and days of thought and planning. The most intense action was that which no eye looked upon. The writing of a single paragraph or a single sentence may be the result of a holy fire from God, yet in regard to the existence of that holy fire the wisest man may not have the least thought.

We speak of *success* as if that were wholly founded upon consequences. A man may be an eternal failure, although his footsteps glitter with gold and his words sparkle with knowledge. Many a man is honored, because favored circumstances connect themselves with his life as if they grew out of it; while many a one is dishonored, because unfavorable circumstances go before him as if they were his own dark shadow. "One of the kings of Persia, possessing a ring set with a valuable jewel, went once on a party of pleasure with some of his particular associates to Mussula Shiraz, and ordered that they should fix the ring on the dome of Asud, with a proclamation that whoever shot an arrow through the circlet of it should have the ring. It chanced that there were at that time four hundred experienced archers attending him, whose arrows all missed: but as a boy was playing on the terrace roof of the monastery, and shooting his arrows at random, the morning breeze conducted one of them through the ring. The prize was bestowed on him, together with other rich gifts."* In this case it was Providence that succeeded, yet the boy received the prize. The experienced archers, though they failed, were really more successful than that fortunate youth. A person who is ignorant of the theory and practice of medicine may gain the credit of curing a dangerous disease, when it was nature itself that did the work. That man is the most successful in the divine kingdom who sets in motion the greatest amount of spiritual power for the glory of God, whatever may be the opinions or rewards of fallen mortals. Whether in solitude one toils and travails, or in the midst of the busy crowd he strives to elevate and to save, his success is to be measured by a divine rule which looks to holy thought, holy action, and holy charac-

* Sheik Saadi, "The Gulistan Or Rose Garden," p. 253.

ter. One may spend a great part of his life in examining the Greek article and the Greek prepositions, and yet by that unappreciated labor he may be quite successful in the sight of Heaven. The variety of work in the system of God is well nigh infinite, and he who attends to any part with wisdom and a pure heart is successful. He may be working deep down at the foundation where few care to go, or he may be finishing the audience room of the great temple of Jehovah,—in either case, if he is doing his best, he is successful. It is not so much the kind of labor, as it is the way of doing it, which gives one character. An angel sent from the courts of God to minister to a dying prisoner, may be doing as great a work as if he had been called to be one of the chief speakers in the congregation of heaven. There are professors in our institutions of learning who are concentrating their power upon a few young men, and by that means doing more for truth and the kingdom of God than many a popular preacher who speaks to thousands. Many a great mind has sowed the seed, and cared for it till it was well nigh ripe,—then a small mind has cut down the harvest, receiving the praise. We may ascertain on the last great day that some pious monk of the dark ages has really done more for the race, than some notable personage whom good men love to honor. It is not place and praise and wealth which establish the fact of success, but it is divine toil and a divine life. "It is said of one of the ancient painters, that although he bestowed immense labor on every one of his productions in the fine arts, he always gave them away; and being asked the reason of it, he replied, 'They are above all price.'" Yes, every form of mental greatness and every deed of love are above all price. It is a very difficult thing to weigh souls. A child that lives its pure life, and then dies, may accomplish more than the titled religionist who reaches the age of three score and ten.

Merit is success. It is itself a good. God sees it if man does not. A thought that has in it worlds of meaning, an act that will brighten in its results forever, a piece of work that seems to reach the ideal of the angels, a prayer that is nothing but prayer, a tear like that which fell from the eye of the Son of God—all these are successful.

Merit is the coin that passes in Heaven. It is stamped with immortality. It has the imprint of eternal youth. Merit knows nothing of shame, for it is beauty itself. It can never be discouraged, for its foundation is truth. Our exact value in the scale of creation is our merit. Just to the extent that we increase our well-being, just to that extent do we increase our worth. Every man, however, is to be judged by the use which he is to the system of God. Paul and Pascal did more for the race than for themselves. To reach out with a kind of omnipresence of excellence is to show our divine lineage.

There is a marked difference between the *outward* and the *inward* Christian. The one fastens upon appearances, loves the sense element, prefers the fire to the still small voice, is charmed too easily by windy action and eloquence. The other demands substance rather than show, delights in that which is spiritual, feels that quiet and solemn emotion is the most godlike. The piety that is inward has greater volume and tone than any other. It sinks down and touches the most secret part of our nature. It has what may be called the principle of *far-reaching-*

ness. The subjective Christian lives at a distance from himself, and so he lives near to God. He is out of sight of the common run of disciples; they being far too much their own followers. Having pitched his tent hard by the gate of heaven, its glories reach him. The period of doubt with him has come to an end: there is simple trust. He has taken God at his word. Hope is unclouded, and the night is gone. Love is like a sun at noon.

An experience of this kind is of the greatest value. Life will never be what it should be without it. The soul will always be anxious, fear will always trouble, until assurance has the ascendency. When the favored time has come, there will be joy such as was never known before. The chains that have held the spirit captive will be broken. The steps are quick and lightsome. The religion of God has become the religion of man. There is a fine spirit of submission. This submission, however, does not mean that the finite is lost in the Infinite; neither does it mean that the will and the feelings are annihilated, leaving nothing but the clear reason to gaze upon the Deity. It is not stoicism making man a piece of iron; not mysticism making man a piece of God. Christian submission implies that the mind yields itself up in holy acquiescence to the Perfect One. Let circumstances be what they may, the soul is satisfied. The real circumstances are those that are spiritual.

That character is never complete which is moulded mainly by outside forces. I care not how active one may be. He may be the model of all that is wanted in the common walks of life. Still if he is led on by nothing but simple observation and visibility, he is not a truly developed person. He may be called by those around him a *practical* man, and may accomplish a great deal in his day and generation, but mere practicality is not sufficient. I am well aware that at the present time this style of life is much thought of. I have no doubt, however, that the great majority of men need a large infusion of the ideal element. This will not make the practical less. It will rather give it more real strength. Is there not a tendency just now, a very strong tendency, to see nothing but *facts?* Is not reason sinking out of sight, because of the pressure of mere events that are narrated? The periodical literature of the day is developing a new form of mind: a form of mind that simply drinks in statements that are made; the argumentative, and the ideal not being cared for. There is danger that men will become mere utilitarians. Every thing has to be weighed and measured; every thing has to be counted off and the price told. I am very much afraid that our whole church life has received a coloring from this low sensational philosophy. All is so attractive because it can be seen and heard and talked about. The more we take up with this life that nourishes itself with observation, practice, and mere chronicling, the more do we sink Christianity into naturalism. Before we are aware of it, we shall have nothing but a system of pale morality. The Christian religion has its glory and value because it has both an ideal and a factual basis: it takes in the absolute and the conditioned, the seen and the unseen. It runs on with the highest and noblest philosophy that the world has ever known. It has to do with the deepest emotions of our nature. It links itself with the loftiest aspirations of the soul. It carries forward the man by an energy which is back of simple nature; an energy which comes from the one supernatural Being of the universe. There is nothing empirical in that higher life which saturates and satisfies God-directed souls. What we want just now is a more profound Christian consciousness, a deeper redemptive experience. We do not wish men to do less, but we wish them to exercise more their entire mental nature, to feel more the great verities of being, to enjoy more the regal blessedness of salvation.

I would have men to be *in* Christ, united to God by a divine life; and then, entering into their own spirits, commune there with eternal and infinite thoughts. I would have them to see that there is a vast world of being within, far greater and better than that which meets the eye of each child of the world. I would have no man to rest satisfied till he comes into contact with the far-reaching convictions of the human spirit; convictions which point the mind away to another sphere than this; to other objects than those that belong to time. No man has waked up to a consciousness of his existence who has not been moved and carried away by emotions deep with eternal significance, by passions that are clearly limitless in their nature, by aspirations that run out to a timeless Being, and by groanings unutterable which human language can neither measure nor define, which nevertheless have a language of their own, a soul-speech giving hints of the First Fair, the Perfect One, the Absolute Good. Our Christian life will always be weak and wayward until we have more of this internal element. It will never have breadth and sweep without this. The experience will always be commonplace and somewhat secular. There will be no heavings of soul which are solemn and sad because of vast conceptions in the mind.

I must say that I love to see an experience so deep that it has something of the indefinite about it. I mind it not if the ideal teaching carries one away into a sphere that is dim because of its magnitude, and even because of its brightness. I am pleased when I see creaturely spirits looking down the eternal deeps of heaven, and beholding clouds of glory measureless to man rolling away in their passage to God. I find a charm in the grandeur of eternal and infinite mysteries. I have no great sympathy for that which is merely limited. Simple rationalism I do not want. It is too narrow and frigid for a soul that was made for eternity and God. I think there is something better than that which we can see; something better than that which we can know. I can not be satisfied with mere facts, however good and however true they may be. There is a kingdom of truth which exists before any of the facts of time, and but for which the facts would have no meaning. There is a great archetypal world made and furnished by the Supreme Mind. I would have men live there more than they do. Life will never be grand and divine unless it is started and guided by celestial ideals. The thought of a law that is eternal and that admits of no change; of a holiness so pure that no sin can ever touch it; of a spiritual beauty that far exceeds the external beauty of the universe; of a scene of order that is only realized in the Godhead; of a blessedness that is without any limitation,—these conceptions enlarge the soul and give power to its life.

We are not to be dazzled by a showy materialism. The greatest powers in the universe are invisible. God is greater than he appears to be. We need more of an inward meditative life. Outward rush and outward goodness are taking the place of deep and holy thoughtfulness. Are men not beginning to love that piety which has the covering of earthliness thrown over it? The covering may be fine or coarse as the taste requires. It may be ornamented with gold or silver, or it may be plain. Still the earthliness is there none the less. Unless I am greatly mistaken, there is a wisdom floating about which can be called by no other name than tact and compromise,—the attempt to sweeten the gospel and make it palatable by encouragements given to ease, and flatteries paid to pride. It does seem as if the philosophy of making men pleased with themselves had reached its utmost limit, and there was need of continuous waves of truthfulness to wash them upon some rock, that there they may see themselves as they are. I wish men to be wiser and better than they appear to be. I would do nothing to increase a fictitious life, but I would do much to help forward that kind of piety which like an artesian well is ever streaming forth, while its deep fountain is never seen. I am glad that there are retiring natures who stay with us for a season and then pass away, whose greatness is never known. They seem like strangers tarrying with us during the short day of our toil, and when the sun goes down they disappear. The beauty of their soul we saw not as they went about with us. Gleams of greatness streamed forth from them as they were departing, and we think of them now as being lofty and lovely in another land. There are scholarly and Christian minds who never find this world just the place that they want. The flower that is planted here never grows with freedom. Its beauty will only be seen in the climes of God. I think the Saviour is the ideal and representative of our theme. How much of hidden greatness he possessed! There was no rule by which he could be measured, no scales by which he could be weighed. His thoughts only reached us like the travelling echoes of God. They seemed like the harmonies of glory that were dying away as they went along the eternal years.

CHAPTER XIV.

BLESSEDNESS AS FLOWING FROM THE RELIGION OF CHRIST.

ALTHOUGH happiness is not the ultimate good, yet unless that which is called the ultimate good ends in happiness, we may well look upon it with suspicion. We have a right to judge of the religion of Christ by its tendency to produce joy. If its natural and necessary result is misery, or if it generates less joy than some other form of life, we may safely condemn it. The case, however, is as near to self-evidence as any one could wish, that religion and blessedness go hand in hand.

I. BLESSEDNESS FROM RIGHT EMOTION.

There is nothing within the whole compass of mind that is higher than religious emotion; nothing that produces such an exalted happiness. The leading faculties, the great truths, the divine persons, all seem to work together in the formation of pure feeling and pure joy. However much a person may have been captivated with inferior pleasures during the days of his worldliness, he now, when a Christian, perceives that the chief blessedness is found in pious emotion. He realizes the truthfulness of the Bible statement: "To be spiritually minded is *life* and *peace.*" This is life in the highest sense, including within itself all good, and that forever; and the peace that belongs to it is that divine repose, called by the significant name "the peace of God."

What joy springs from the sense of *freedom.* The simple fact that the will, which has been held to a course of disobedience for years, is now made obedient—that is blessedness. A new channel of joy has been opened by this means around the soul. Wherever the liberated will goes, there goes with it an exalted pleasure. The very sound of its footsteps is happiness, and the beating of its pulse of life is joy. The vast number of original acts of goodness that have appeared since the will was delivered from its bondage, and the host of sins that have been trampled under foot since the same redemptive moment, awaken a multitude of pleasant emotions. There are habits of righteousness which maintain a solid peace, and pure states of soul that are instinct with joy. Passions and propensities do not master the will as formerly. The power of holy necessity is felt to a certain extent, and this composes the mind.

Love itself is joy. It is doubtful whether there is another feeling of the soul which, in its movement, is so much like happiness as love. To say that we love the good, is to say that we delight in it. If an object pleases me, I have an affection for it: if I have an affection for an object, it pleases me. Love, then, is blessedness; from its nature it forms a heaven. And inasmuch as it takes in the highest excellency, and is really the most comprehensive feeling of the soul, it furnishes a joy that is ineffable. "Desire and delight," says John Howe, "are but two acts of love, diversified only by the distance or presence of the same object: which, when 'tis distant, the soul, acted and prompted by love, desires, moves towards it, pursues it; when present and attained, delights in it, enjoys it, stays upon it, satisfies itself in it, according to the measure of goodness it finds there. Desire is therefore love in motion; delight is love in rest."* Whatever may be the kind of love that is exercised, it is embosomed in happiness. Let one be grateful for a favor received, inclined to love the giver more than the gift, in such a case there is joy. To be in a constant state of thankfulness is to be constantly happy. If a feeling of holy sympathy is exercised, that sends vibrations of pleasure through the heart; and if the soul goes forth in universal good-will, it has a divine joy. If our kindness extends to those who hate us, forgiving and blessing at the same time, we have a wealth of happiness.

We should bring ourselves to that point in our spiritual history when religious emotion shall, so to speak, *engross* our attention. There is a vast number of things connected with our earthly condition, which will be stripped from us the moment we leave the body. It is surely not wise to allow these mundane characteristics to grasp the immortal spirit. When the ransomed soul enters eternity it will be compelled to

---

* "Blessedness of the Righteous," chap. iv.

face pure emotion, that being the prime reality. If delight is not found in that, it will not not be found anywhere. In a state of marked singleness the naked spirit shall live in the region of mind; each hour as it passes making the life of emotion the one life. We should test and try ourselves while here, in order to see whether our chief delight is found in simple spiritual realities. Although the Christian soul while in the body has many material interests which occupy its attention, and many things which tend to render doubtful the supremacy of the religious principle, yet when that soul is freed from its prison, it will hasten to God by the force of spiritual gravitation, the ascendency of holiness showing itself at once. In the region of souls matter will be nothing: mind with its goodness and blessedness will be all.

"It is not in that he is a man," says Aristotle, "that any one enjoys this life, but in so far as there is any thing *divine* in him." That soul which has the greatest amount of the divine will have the greatest amount of holy emotion and blessedness. When we take into consideration the ascending scale of finite minds throughout the universe, the highest minds must differ exceedingly from the lowest in the quality of *fineness*. Some natures may have such delicacy about them, such divinity, that their enjoyment is far beyond any thing that we can imagine. There may be minds which from the very beginning of their history spring forth into unwonted excellence, and during all their upward course live in a region of joy that is far beyond any that we can ever experience. They are cut out of such fine material, formed as it were of the life and radiance of God, that they seem to live in a divine sphere, the nearest to the Deity of any of the creatures that he has ever made. Great volumes of love and gladness move across their being, as if the pulsations of God thrilled them, and as if his beatitudes went through their soul, furnishing a joy that is unspeakable and full of glory.

II. BLESSEDNESS FROM RIGHT ACTIVITY.

The soul was evidently designed for action. It is always occupied. Even during hours of what we call idleness, it is not idle. It is thinking about this or that, feeling about this or that. We can not make the soul not to act. It will keep working whatever we may do. The mind has contents and materials of its own; and these it will use when it can find nothing else to use. The imagination will be forming its ideas into new shapes; building castles one hour, and demolishing them the next. The law of association is intensely active. Deeds long forgotten are remembered, and emotions once felt are felt over again. It is astonishing how the mind will work. It is assuredly a power; a force acting forever.

If we watch men we can see they have the consciousness that joy comes from activity. They will tell you that they always feel the happiest when they are doing something. If they have no special work on hand, they will invent that which will take the place of it. They will start some amusement, will converse with each other, will visit, will rush off into what is called pleasure, will read the news of the day, will dream and plan and hope as fancy dictates. Let thinking be of the right character and carried to the right extent, and a very sweet peace will be the result of it. Let the will be the faithful executive of the soul, governing and guiding all its movements in the way of righteousness, and as a matter of certainty the purest kind of joy will settle down upon it. Let any man spend a whole day in working for God, self-forgetful during all that time, and, as a consequence, happiness must come to the soul like the Sabbath of heaven. The very light as it darts through space seems to be happy. The stars sparkle in the evening sky with gladness. The planets wheel their way without any jar as if they were the chariots of God. The great systems journey onward forever, peace bearing them company in their march. All these seem to image forth that joy which comes to active souls.

When we speak of the activity of man, that may mean less or more, according as it is moderate or rapid. If the joy is to be rich, there must be great force about the activity. If the mind is profoundly occupied with the most exalted themes, and intent upon the highest style of well-doing, the blessedness will be both great and pure. If there is nothing but a species of mediocrity about the soul's movements, the joy will partake of that quality. To an uncritical observer, every thing about the mind and the man may seem to be in good condition; there may be a tangibleness and pleasantness connected with all that is done; but the difficulty may be that the action is too feeble, and the joy too insipid in its quality. Christian knowledge and Christian life may be so popularized that they will neither have heights nor depths about them. Viewing thought and character, however, as two great activities, they must swell out into living mountain ranges, forming, in fact, palaces, cathedrals, and mansions of life in the soul, and not the mere level plains of goodness and peace. There are surely philosophic and saintly eminences where the soul may have fore-tastes of heavenly glory, and where ineffable joys are felt as they could be felt nowhere else. The total activity of the average Christian mind has not sufficient power and compass, and the joy has not that celestial flavor which should always characterize it. When good souls strike out upon their march in the great kingdom of eternity, what a volume of power they will call into exercise, and how divine the blessedness as they sweep along the infinite spaces of life! The joy of heavenly minds will resemble the joy of God; there being no motion of pain during all the passage of endless time. Saved men will have entered upon a new and wondrous life; the entire soul will thrill with power; the highest form of benevolence will be exercised; and a happiness will be enjoyed that reaches the true standard of excellence.

III. BLESSEDNESS FROM RIGHT PASSIVITY.

There is such a thing as righteous *being* as well as righteous *doing*. For instance, to be humble,—how much of peace that brings to the soul! Then to be gentle and meek, amiable and quiet, uncomplaining and teachable,—what a wealth of character is found in these holy states of mind, and how pure the repose which results from them! Indeed, when one thinks of the matter, he is led to decide that passive goodness is the very substratum and heart of all true peace. A person who is chiefly active, having but a small amount of passive spirituality, is not a true man, neither does he have that volume of joy which belongs to the well-balanced mind. There are times when we wish to be let alone, wish to be quiet; and during such seasons we seem to be bathed in a heavenly fountain of peace. The moments glide away as if they were the echoes of God, and the angels seem to converse with us in the language of souls.

There are fine, serene days when we want to sit down upon the bank of a stream and watch it as it flows by us, looking at the scenery around, and feeling quite happy with all that we behold. The very idea of *rest* seems to bring along with it the idea of *quietness*. Noise disturbs us; as if we wanted to dwell in a serene land; far away from the tumults of life; at peace with God with nothing to annoy. We love a quiet Sabbath day, as if with such a day we come near to the rest that we need. How saintly men have calmly wondered at the life of Christ! The beauty of that life; its freedom from all wildness; the praying through the long night; the gentle speech to children and men; the mysterious sorrow that always hung around him;

his sweet submission; his strange death,—how all these affect us and soften us just by putting ourselves in a line with them!

Men who have toiled for years at some calling think of a time when they shall retire from business. They are thus feeling round for the quiet joy which they need. There is a craving in all souls for repose; and they shall never be well till they find it. They keep dreaming about it; having an inkling of the place where it dwells. We think of men reaching home after a long absence, of the sick gaining health when the balmy days of spring are come, of the persecuted finding peace, and the dying Christian finding rest in the bosom of God. When we see a ship anchored in a quiet bay after a stormy passage, we think of the joy that comes to souls in a region of calmness and silent life.

Surely there is a time when the healthy mind can rest. I can not think that we were made simply for ceaseless labor,—under the stretch and strain of eternal toil. There is a passive season of great enjoyment, when the beatitudes of glory circulate through our whole being, and no want disturbs us during the passage of the silent hours. We seem to enter into the rest of God, and the peace that passeth all understanding comes to the soul. The great difficulty with the human spirit upon earth is, that we can not stop and look into it with any degree of comfort. We only become conscious of our unhappiness and sin when we try to live in the soul. Hence men rush into outward activities, keep the mind fixed upon them, finding in that way that they lose sight of the unrest of the soul. Now, surely, this can not be the right way. I must reach a point when I can feel happy in communing with my own spirit. I must be able to look into every chamber, go through every hall, try and test every part of my nature, and find that happiness meets me wherever I go and wherever I stay. The idea that I must steadily gaze at some outward object, as the only way to escape from inward misery, is a fearful thought. This is mere deception; simply living in the midst of the unreal. The soul must be cured: then to look into it will be a sweet joy. The men who are in Heaven are not men who have to turn the wheels of action eternally, in order to enjoy peaceful emotions. They can abate during some divine hour. They can face themselves during that hour. They can see and feel that all is right within. Resting in the midst of finished being, they can find rest.

IV. BLESSEDNESS FROM THE ATTAINMENT OF A RIGHT END.

The insects that play in the air on a summer's day seem to be happy. We naturally think that they have reached some end, and as a consequence of it are touched with joy. When we walk through a garden and see the flowers that are smiling there, and catch the sweet perfume that fills the surrounding air, we have an impression that these flowers have attained a distinct end, and so in their own way they are in a state of peace. A tree that is full of blossoms, and by and by is full of fruit, we look upon as an image of a good soul, and can not help thinking that that tree has a kind of native gladness about it. The birds that come to us in the spring and stay with us through all the summer, have a certain round of duties which they perform in that time, and in all that round of duties they evidently have a great deal of pleasure.

They attend to their young with wonderful care; and when they have moments of rest, they sing most sweetly the hymn which God taught them. The bee that toils so faithfully, must also be toiling pleasantly. Having found the treasure that it wants, it rests.

What a fine consciousness one has when he realizes that the great question of life is *settled*. The soul has committed itself into the hands of the Infinite Redeemer. It is now set for an eternal life by all the steadiness of an absolute choice. Comprehending this state of things, there is peace. A heavy burden has dropped off from the soul: there is the feeling of relief. One seems to himself as if he had just begun to live. The nightmare of life is gone. The void of the soul is partly filled. The whole nature seems to feel the effect of the great change, as if spring had suddenly come after the long winter, and the golden day after the night of darkness. Throughout all the city of the soul there is joy. The bells ring. The sound of pleasant music falls upon the ear. Prayer ascends and praise. God listens and loves. A divine benediction comes down upon the soul. "I was so happy," says

Bogatzky, "that I would have been willing to remain shut up in my closet during life, provided I could frequently enjoy such seasons. A true light sprang up in my soul, and I then learned that Christianity was something living, powerful, blessed, and altogether different from the world's notion of it."*

There is the joy which connects itself with *pardon.* To realize that the collective sins of the past are gone, is most blessed. To feel that as far as law is concerned, we are the same as if we had always kept it; that the angels in heaven are not more secure than the justified soul,—to feel thus is happiness. To accept of the entire salvation of the Godman is to enter into joy, very much as if one had entered into heaven. Not only is the past emptied of its sin, but the future is emptied of its terror. As memory looks back, it is soothed with the balm of life: as conscience looks forward, it is calmed by the Peacemaker of men. Faith and Hope go hand in hand through the journey of time: the one quieting the soul in the midst of the

---

* Hagenbach, "Hist. of the Church in the 18th and 19th centuries," vol. i., p. 137.

storm—the other pointing with the finger to the open gates of heaven.

Whenever we undertake any great work, and persevere till it is finished, we in such a case feel happy. If we have labored for months to lead a man to Christ, and finally he trusts himself in the hands of that great person, we are full of joy. If in spite of much opposition we have been able to start an organization that will benefit the bodies and souls of men, we are delighted. If we have conquered a leading sin, or have broken up some vicious habit, we are happy in the attainment of such an end. If by skill and industry we have saved a sufficiency of money upon which to live, and now during the remainder of life can simply work for God,—an end so good as that will be exceedingly pleasant. If we have written a book after years of labor, and that book will bless men when we are dead, there is much joy in the realization of such an end. When Dr. Adam Clarke had finished his commentary on the Bible, he added these words:—

"Like travellers, when they see their native soil,
Writers rejoice to terminate their toil."

If I set out to visit a country that I have never seen, but by reason of some catastrophe I never reach it, I am disappointed and grieved. If I enter upon a branch of business, but fail in it because men have deceived and defrauded me, I can not be pleased. Even if I have a great thought that is shaded with uncertainty, I am troubled. If I have longings of soul that are not met by a suitable object, I am unhappy. I can see that my nature craves something of infinite moment, and if that something is not found I am restless. If my soul is always burdened, feverish, and faint, I have not reached the great end. Joy is simply the bright conclusion of goodness: grief is simply the dark conclusion of sin.

There is a *seeming pleasure* which may arise from an end that was supposed to be within our reach. The soul is in the midst of a dream. While the dream lasts, all appears real. The person may seem to himself to be sailing down a beautiful stream, expecting to reach his home at the close of the day. The banks are covered with verdure. Flocks of sheep are feeding upon the sides of the hills. Quiet villages are seen here and there in the distance. Hard by are the ruins of an ancient city, and an artist is sketching the scene from the top of a rock. Birds of gay plumage are flying around. Groups of men, women, and children, are seated in the midst of a grove, and a psalm of praise like to that which they sing in heaven falls upon the ear. An extended highway stretches onward, along which happy companies are walking. The sun has passed its noon. The heat scorches not. The air is pleasant. The person is still sailing down the stream. A cloud covers the sky. The wind blows. A mighty cataract is at hand. Down that the man is swept. He is lost; lost in the midst of a dream.

Whenever we reach the *permanent* we rest. There are few things that so impress the mind in regard to the present state, as the fact of change. Nothing seems to abide. We live upon the surface of a decayed world. The perishable is inscribed upon it, and upon the heavens that are over it. There is a fickleness in the hopes, wishes, and opinions of men. We demand that which is fixed. Eternal truth,—how the soul can build upon it! An immutable promise,—how comforting to the troubled mind! The everlasting God,—how the trusting spirit can rest on him! Unchanging goodness,—how it satisfies the soul! Only that which is at rest can give rest. The true and the divine have a peace of their own, and so they quiet the mind.

If we attain to the *beautiful* in Christianity, there is peace. The happiness which springs from this source does not seem to be boisterous: it is rather tranquilizing in its nature. The texture of it is fine and finished. We can say that the soul is pleased; that a sweet composure has settled down upon it; that a divine serenity spreads over it. Purity of heart is not dazzling, but chaste and refined.

V. BLESSEDNESS FROM A RIGHT STATE OF ONENESS.

Every intelligent person knows what pleasure there is in finding a principle that will unite a number of apparently contradictory things. Simplicity and pleasure are connected with the study of trees and flowers, because so many of them can be reduced to one leading characteristic. It is the same with the study of the animal creation. There appears to be no end to the variety of beasts, birds, insects, and fishes; yet they are all classified according to a few simple principles. As to the human race with all their differences of color, form, language, and location, we yet find that "God has made of *one blood* all nations that dwell upon the face of the earth." In fact all theological and philosophical systems are feeling round for a principle of unity. The mind is eager to escape from confusion and disharmony. What a wonderful manifestation of singleness is the law of gravitation: no particle of matter free from its power. The dust that enters the infant's eye and the most distant planet that sails in solitude through space, alike governed by this one principle. What a relief also to the serious mind that wherever we look and wherever we go, we simply find one God. The satisfaction we thus have when we reach oneness, shows how well it suits our nature.

Let the soul be in a state of oneness *with itself*, and it will as matter of course feel happy. As the Christian man struggles to overcome pride and selfishness, evil thoughts and malicious feelings, he approaches unity. The effort to bear up under the trials of life, to be quiet in the midst of provocation, to resist the tempting influences of a day, prepares the soul for that pure state which ends in peace. Every holy action performed and prayer offered; each act of repentance and act of faith; the courage that inspires and the hope that cheers; the noble purpose and the longing after righteousness,—all lead to oneness. The fact that the various faculties are animated by one divine life, gives promise of victory. The chief powers of the mind are thus leagued together. They seek one common end. When there is a single governing principle in the soul, this will naturally draw all the other principles to it as to a centre. Opposite forces will in course of time lose their strength. They will be brought to a stand. They will change masters, and submit to ultimate authority. They will move pleasantly around the great centre. The severed parts will come together again. There will be oneness, and along with that *wholeness*: no mental and moral schism any more. The soul is one, as Adam before the fall, as Christ in his purity, as

God in his love. The result of this is blessedness.

There is such a thing as *proportion*. When we look at a human body we see nothing one-sided. The arms are of the same length; the hands are shaped alike; one eye does not differ from another; one side of the face does not project outward, while the other side sinks; the whole body is finely balanced. In all the animal races the same fact of symmetry appears. In the plant kingdom there is also a complete order in the different parts of the different organisms. Even in the formation of crystals the most beautiful kind of proportion is manifested. A grain of salt, a drop of rain, a flake of snow, the icicles hanging pendant from the trees on a winter's morning, all point to a principle of oneness. Perhaps the different rays of light are modelled according to a law of celestial order, being a kind of divine images of well-proportioned souls. Surely the human spirit needs to be right on every side. A great intellect with feeble emotion, or great emotion with a feeble intellect, strikes us badly. We demand that every part and feature of the mind shall be properly balanced.

Having gone as far as this, the soul must now be in a state of oneness *with God*. He is the chief good. The creaturely spirit is an insipid and meaningless thing when living away from him. As the soul was fashioned for God, and bears about with it a divine likeness, it can not feel well without him. Its human and temporal side is nothing. The mere natural tie which binds the creature to the Creator can neither start purity nor peace. Development in blessedness is no more possible than development in holiness while the soul is estranged from God.

Every faculty must be in a state of unison with the Deity. The *intellect* must be satisfied with the *truth* of God. Many of the divine ideas are bright, and many are dark. With the one class we are pleased, and with the other class we are perplexed. This shows that there is not complete harmony between the mind of man and the mind of God. Even though we may know but little respecting an Infinite Being, yet if that little is sound, the soul works in a healthy manner. True blessedness is not possible with false conceptions. There is such a thing as intellectual joy, the repose of a well-balanced understanding, the fruition that comes to the logical and intuitional faculties when they find nothing but eternal truth. If now the *feelings* are brought into a state of oneness with God, how divine the blessedness of the soul! Every feeling matching with every truth; rounded and intensified by every truth, —the heart therefore full of joy. Let the *will* now be ready to answer to the demands of pure emotion, and peace will follow as matter of consequence from the working of that faculty. The will taking the entire soul and giving that to God is blessedness. The Divine Being is now "the unending end."

The perfected soul is also in a state of oneness *with the holy intelligences* of heaven, and by that means the joy is complete. They work and worship together with the utmost harmony; and through the whole of the eternal day they shall be one without any break. They may rise higher and higher in their separate personalities, branch off in different directions as their minds lead, still no schism appears in the great family of God. In sweetest peace they abide through all the years. Heart beats responsive with heart, and soul touches soul in the glorious commonwealth of the celestial. Whether they walk beside the river of God, or watch and wait at the city gates of life, or fly on some great embassy to distant worlds, they still are one. Whatever the offices they hold, differing as souls differ, no envy eats into any heart, nor does jealousy trouble any spirit among them all. Contention for place and power is seen not there. Each goes where wisdom sends, and dwells in peace where love delights to stay. Some are quite royal in their flights, as if with the noblest they could fly and weary not; reaching the great kingdoms of light, the highest that are found among the realms of God. Others lower down are pleased to live and love, working there in sacred ministry as time runs by. No meanness characterizes any soul or any sphere. The lowest are kings and priests to God: the highest are never more than that. No line of discord is seen on any face, nor murmur of discontent heard from any lip. The joy of the Lord sparkles in every eye, and hope beckons the spirit onward without a cloud. They are all dwelling in the midst of day, dwelling in the midst of love; so that disunion can not find a corner in which to grow in any soul.

Whatever is pleasant upon earth will be heightened in pleasantness in heaven. Our purest friendships will be still purer there. No fine trait will be lost, no truth left behind, no beauty that will not embellish the souls of the saved. The collective purity and blessedness of time is but a dream of heaven. How souls will rest when they enter the country of God! No darkness will cloud them, nor fear annoy them through all their days. They will be ascending forever on the wings of love, and joy shall warm their heart in all their journey of peace. No pain shall wound them as they pass onward, but they shall be happy with the happiness of God, and life shall be before them through the ceaseless years. Whether in companies or alone, the soul shall be at rest. The time will pass away in the midst of gladness, for the eternal day shall be full of God. His light shall be in their souls, and hope shall ever be shining above them like a sun. They shall faint not again, nor be sad. The burden of sin is gone, and perfect joy is found.

Blessed state! How in our toil and battle we long to reach it. Contradictions strike into us; confusion surrounds us; we long for the unity and repose of the endless life. How in our dreams we think of that divine age of bliss, and of the people who fellowship in peace in the temple of the Lord. Their worship has no imperfection, their work no weariness, their joy no pain. They will keep on with the march of infinite time; and when a small eternity has rolled away they will be great with the greatness of God Heaven will be always around them, always within them, and so they live and rest in the midst of eternal goodness,

All hail, thou wondrous Christianity! What blessedness thou bringest to souls! Age weakens not thy power. Eternal youth is stamped upon thy brow. Men have sought thy destruction; but thou hast no death. Thou hast quickened into life uncounted millions; giving them hope in the hour of despair, and joy to gladden them through all the length of their way. The most wicked thou hast changed with thy love; making them bright with the glory of the Lord, and citizens of a kingdom that shall never end. When we enter the valley of death thy voice shall comfort us, and thy smile shall radiate around our souls. Crossing the river thou shalt be with us; conducting us home to the palace of life; making us complete for evermore. Noble religion of the Crucified! I devote my all to thee. May my eye lose its lustre, my tongue its speech, my arm its strength, if I forget thee. Thou art all that I have. I sink into eternal darkness without thee. Christ and Christianity are my stay. I want no more.

THE END.

www.ingramcontent.com/pod-product-compliance
Lightning Source LLC
Chambersburg PA
CBHW021205230426
43667CB00006B/568